The Rhythm of Grief

The Rhythm of Grief

A Memoir of Love, Loss and Learning to Breathe Again

Elizabeth Jean Braun

Braun House Press

Copyright © 2026 Braun House Press

The moral right of the author has been asserted.

All rights reserved.
No part of this publication may be reproduced, stored in a retrieval system, or transmitted, in any form or by any means, without the prior permission in writing of the publisher, nor be otherwise circulated in any form of binding or cover other than that in which it is published and without a similar condition including this condition being imposed on the subsequent purchaser.

Published by Braun House Press

ISBN 979-8-9944071-0-3

Cover design by Myda Iamiceli

Edited by: Corinne Keller, Anne Morris, and Tracy Young

Audiobook narrated by Elizabeth Jean Braun

Audiobook production: Anne Morris

Typesetting services by BOOKOW.COM

For George, who loved me so well.

An Invitation

Why write a book about grief?

One night, slowly sipping a glass of red wine, I was journaling about my feelings while sitting on a dark brown leather reclining loveseat that my husband had purchased several years before his death.

I could not stand this piece of furniture while he was alive, yet it is now a loveseat I have learned to cherish.

On that night, five years after my husband's death, I found myself reflecting on how grief had woven its way into my everyday life. I considered some of the collateral beauty I have experienced because of this grief.

I was familiar with the term "collateral damage." But it wasn't until George and I were in a New York City hotel room, about seven months before he died, that I first heard the phrase "collateral beauty." We were watching a movie by that title.

"Beauty" from death—an oxymoron in its truest form.

As I continued journaling my feelings, desires, and goals, I could see that many of the good parts of my present-day life stemmed from a pivotal moment, when my life was shredded beyond recognition, the moment my husband died.

The good stuff. The parts of my life I was genuinely enjoying... that was the collateral beauty.

Grief introduced me to unexpected connections, new ways of thinking, and a deeper understanding of myself. It opened doors I never imagined would be connected to loss.

My grief is real and will remain with me for the rest of my life. I find comfort in that thought, because it means my husband is still with me. This makes me feel human, makes me smile, and fills my soul with warmth so that when I awaken each morning, I can feel a sense of happiness.

This invitation is a beginning. What follows is a rhythm of grief. My rhythm. It is offered with the hope that it may help you find yours.

***

Journal Entry – August 2025 (Seven years after his death)

As I think of my grief, I feel it has morphed me. I no longer know who I would be without it.

***

Contents

Chapter 1

The Beginning

Me, Him, Us and How Grief Began

* * *

I hold it true, whate'er befall;

I feel it, when I sorrow most;

'Tis better to have loved and lost

Than never to have loved at all.

–Alfred Lord Tennyson

* * *

George and I enjoyed sitting on our back porch swing most mornings. After twenty-three years of marriage, we still struggled to find the perfect rhythm. I would swing too slowly; he, too fast. But each day, we found a pace that suited us both.

We liked our coffee with so much sugar and cream that it barely resembled coffee at all. Teasing each other about it, we'd smile and take another sip. Sometimes we talked quietly or just listened to the sounds of the day waking up. There was no urgency.

We had routines like that, small, steady rituals that bound our lives together. Morning coffee. Afternoon cocktails. Quiet glances and grins that said more than words ever could. We were a team, practiced and comfortable in the shared language of a long marriage.

He called me Honey Bunny. I called him the same.

We had built a life that felt solid. It was shaped by an incredible amount of laughter, hard work, shared responsibility, and a deep, abiding respect for one another. It wasn't perfect—but it was ours, and it was good.

I didn't know then how much those ordinary moments would come to matter.

I didn't realize how soon I would count time by breaths, heartbeats, or ten-second intervals. That I would search for him in quiet rooms and still talk to him long after his body was gone.

But this story does not begin with his death.

It begins with our life.

The life and love story I shared with George Fredrick Braun was anything but conventional.

We met later in our lives; not that we were old, but we were both wary following difficult first marriages. Our backgrounds and childhoods could not have been much more different.

Me

I was born in New Jersey, the fourth of five children in the early 1960s. As a family, we moved almost every seven years. No, I was not an Army brat; our family just moved around a lot.

My father worked outside the home, and for most of my childhood, my mother was a housewife–until the family finances collapsed around 1976.

I had a 1960s version of a traditional childhood: a mother, father, one brother, three sisters, and a family dog. It was well known that Danny, our German shorthaired pointer, belonged to Dad.

He fiercely protected, trained, and fed Danny. As a child, I sometimes wished I were Danny.

Dad's version of affection toward his children was a rough pat on the head and the affectionate name "Meathead" was used for all six of us (five kids and the dog).

Corporal punishment was, for the most part, phased out after the first two children, Jim and Cindy. It was replaced with what we kids referred to as "the death stare" and accompanied by the mumbled threat, "You'll be picking shoe leather out of your ass for the next week."

He muttered this whenever we were doing something that bothered him, which happened to be quite often. It took time, but I came to understand that Dad loved us the only way he knew how.

Mom was our safe spot; she made us feel smart and loved. She deflected our hurt feelings from Dad's stares and threats with humor and kind, uplifting words. We cherished spending time with her–playing games, telling jokes, and listening to her laugh.

When I think of my childhood, this is my memory lane: listening to the classic music of Three Dog Night and the Beatles.

I used to love listening to my mom sing along with Mitch Miller and Bing Crosby. That love of music followed me into school, where I joined the chorus, and eventually into adulthood, when I learned to play the guitar–something that would come to mean more to me than I could have known at the time.

On television, we watched The Mary Tyler Moore Show and The Flintstones. In the neighborhood, we caught lightning bugs, rode bicycles with banana seats, and played outside until we heard the family dinner bell.

We had a roof over our heads, but money was scarce, and our extended family sent us boxes of hand-me-down clothes each summer.

All of the children left home as soon as we could (except for Lori, the youngest–she stayed the longest).

It was late in my sophomore year of high school, and I was on track to graduate a year early. Jim, my big brother, and my older sisters, Cindy and Frances Ann, had already flown the coop. My departure came just as the "seven-year itch" was knocking at my parents' door again. It was spring 1980 when they decided to move across the state, and I simply refused to go. I was sixteen.

Had I moved with Mom, Dad, and Lori, none of my night-school classes would have been completed. I would have had to attend my senior year of high school in person and at a brand-new school.

Not long after I went out on my own, I made one of those decisions that altered the trajectory of my life, not in a good way. I married a man significantly older than me who had also been my high school algebra teacher.

By 1992 the marriage was failing and we were living about a hundred miles away from most of my family.

Late one afternoon, my sister Fran called to let me know that our mother was seriously ill. She was later diagnosed with lung and kidney cancer… two primary cancers, not metastatic.

Shortly after the news, I moved to live in the same town as my parents. When my first husband refused to relocate with me, I began my divorce proceedings.

A little over a year later, my mother was holding her own through her cancer treatment. My divorce was final and I had met and married the man who intentionally became the love of my life.

I went from some of the lowest of low times to being absolutely high on life.

George Fredrick Braun– Childhood
George was born in 1951, and his beginning was both traumatic and chaotic.

He was delivered in the toilet of an old second-story apartment in Pittsburgh, Pennsylvania. While his mother screamed in hysteria, his fourteen-year-old uncle Fred pulled him from the water, saving his life.

George's earliest memories were painful. He remembered being placed in an orphanage and told it was because his mother had been in a terrible automobile accident. George recalled looking out of the window at the orphanage driveway, waiting and hoping for his mother's return.

He remembered receiving letters from his mother that the nuns would read to him. George treasured the letters and hid them under his bed mattress. At one point, a hurricane forced the orphanage to evacuate and the letters were lost. George remembered the frantic and uncontrollable crying that followed.

His mother eventually picked him up and took him to Miami. He spent his life from age three through high school in South Miami Beach, Florida. George never learned who his father was.

Before he was old enough for school, he and his mother moved frequently from place to place, usually in the middle of the night, to avoid confrontations with landlords when rent money was scarce.

Even with working two jobs, she struggled. They lived in boarding houses and George often went hungry. He learned to forage for recently discarded food in the garbage cans of nearby restaurants. George would search through furniture cushions for coins and try to keep a low profile.

Before leaving for work, his mother would call the boarding house office and leave the phone off the hook so George could speak into the receiver if he became frightened while she was gone.

Because of this instability, George had very few keepsakes or pictures from his childhood.

Still, he did recall a few fun memories: attending Our Lady of the Hills summer camp for boys in North Carolina and visiting the 1964 World's Fair in New York City.

* * *

Excerpt from Lexi's (George's oldest daughter) memorial words at George's Celebration of Life:

"You see, my grandma did the best she could, but my dad didn't grow up in a family where he knew he was loved, that he was welcome, that he was safe, much less having fun. So he spent his entire life making sure everyone around him knew that they were important, they were loved, they were safe, and that they had fun."

* * *

The seed for George becoming a firefighter was planted during those formative years in South Miami.

One day, he saw a fire engine screaming down the road on the way to a fire call, with the firefighters hanging off the tailboard pulling on their bunker gear.

George was playing outside, and as the engine drew closer and slowed for a turn, a fire helmet fell off the truck and rolled to the side of the street. He ran over to the helmet, scooped it up, and immediately went home to hide it.

That helmet remains hanging in my home today. Perhaps the helmet should have been returned…but I cherish it nonetheless.

* * *

Together
December 6, 1993, I met George Braun, a firefighter and driver-operator with the department, at a celebration for the municipal fire department's combat-challenge team, where my sister Cindy was being honored. He was there as the department's photographer.

Our initial meeting, to downplay it, was electric. Later the following week, I met his two children (Lexi and Bailey) and subsequently fell in love with all three of them.

We purchased a house in July 1994 and were married in October 1994, just ten months after meeting.

Then, in 2002, with support from my family, I changed my nearly sixteen-year career in education to enter the fire service, something that would become part of our family's story.

After ten years of trying to create a child together, George and I adopted our little girl, Emma Jean, in 2005. We could not have been happier.

As our family grew, as we developed our individual careers, and as the years passed, we navigated life's many trials and triumphs together. We were happy.

Truly happy.

* * *

George's Passion and Professional Life
Honey Bunny was our nickname for each other from about the third week we started dating.

We chose it so we wouldn't accidentally slip and call each other by an ex-spouse's name… a private little joke that made us smile. What may have sounded lighthearted on the surface carried a deeper meaning for us, rooted in intention, respect, and the life we were building together.

The more I got to know George, the more he amazed me. I admired his professional drive, determination, humor, deep love, compassion, and empathy. Shortly after we met, he was promoted to lieutenant within the fire department.

Many career firefighters, due to the typical type "A" personality and the shift schedule, have a second job. In that respect, George was no different. His second career was teaching fire suppression, Hazardous Materials, and fire leadership classes across the state of Florida.

Firefighters throughout the country have, for decades, brandished the remnants of working fires: melted shields and the smell of smoke-stained bunker gear as badges of honor. The dirtier the gear, the tougher and more accomplished the firefighter was thought to be.

Exposure to smoke and soot was accepted as part of the job, never imagining the long-term health consequences that would later be linked to cancer and other life-altering illnesses.

George was ahead of his time. From the moment he joined the fire service in 1980, he began researching new, improved, and safer methods of firefighting. It was his innate driving force to find more accurate or more efficient ways to do any task.

Long before the dangers of smoke and soot were widely acknowledged, George understood that protecting firefighters meant protecting their future. He was teased by his co-workers because he kept his helmet shiny and his bunker gear free of soot and smoke remnants. Nonetheless, he continued to read the research and encouraged his co-workers and firefighters statewide to pay attention and do the same.

In 2007, George retired from firefighting as a lieutenant with 27 years of service to the community.

Although he decided to retire from the department, he did not "feel done" with the fire service. George continued teaching professional firefighting classes and began applying to other departments at a higher rank that would allow him to more influence to make change within the fire service.

It took five years, but he found his dream job. He applied to and was hired by Reedy Creek Improvement District (Reedy Creek). Reedy Creek serves Disney World and the immediate surrounding properties providing firefighting, emergency medical, and fire prevention services.

His new job was to build a training program from the ground up. Reedy Creek gave him the support and funding to fulfill this mission, and he did. He was proud of his work, and I remain proud of him and all he accomplished.

* * *

Excerpt from Cindy's (my big sister) memorial words at George's Celebration of Life:

"George was kind, caring, loving, creative, and imaginative; no wonder he loved Disney so much. Everything he did, he tried to make it better, more fun, and more interesting."

* * *

Our Life During His Dream Job

His dream job came with a steep price: travel away from home. Each Monday George drove from Gainesville to Orlando and returned home on the weekends.

His promise to me was that this would be a temporary situation. In a few years, he would "really retire," and we would be able to spend more time together doing what we loved… thinking up house projects, completing them together, and teasing our youngest as she helped.

By then, George's older children, Lexi and Bailey, were busy building their own lives, so the three of us, George, Emma Jean and I, were inseparable from Friday night until Monday morning, when George had to drive back to Orlando.

Even with the distance, we stayed connected. We spoke on the phone every night. We wrote each other postcards. And when the weekends arrived, we guarded our time together with a vengeance.

The Beginning of the End… The Diagnosis

On April 14, 2016, George came home early from Orlando, explaining that Reedy Creek Health Services sent him home after his annual physical because he was in "A-Fib." Atrial Fibrillation is a disorganized heart rhythm that can cause one to feel tired with little to no exertion.

George came straight to my fire station, where I was working as a fire lieutenant and a paramedic. I performed a 12-lead electrocardiogram on him. Sure enough, not only was he in A-Fib, he was also simultaneously in Atrial Flutter, another type of disorganized heart rhythm.

He spent the night in the hospital emergency department.

In May 2016, while shaving, George felt a lump on the left side of his neck. Two weeks later, the lump was still there.

After a round of antibiotics, an ultrasound, and a CT scan, he had a biopsy. The diagnosis was delivered July 3, 2016. George had squamous cell carcinoma. The point of origin was never found.

After the physician explained the diagnosis, we walked to the car hand-in-hand.

We sat in our seats, buckled up—literally and figuratively—and began the heartbreaking conversation about how we were going to tell our children that our lives had just forever changed.

Nothing would ever be the same.

Not ever again.

Chapter 2

Stopped in My Tracks

Finding Meaning in Moments That Change Everything

When the sky is falling, you might expect there would be no time to plan, only react.

Not for our household.

After the cancer diagnosis, George and I stopped everything to do just that: make a plan. It was an all-out war plan against the cancer that had invaded our lives.

Our dining room became The War Room. In this room we mustered our efforts to conquer the unconquerable. All of the customary calming artwork was removed and replaced with calendar pages that contained appointments, school pick-up and drop-off schedules, meal plans, shopping plans, childcare plans, animal care schedules, and emergency contact numbers. Strategically placed around them were affirming messages of love, and reassurance we were going to kill the cancer. On the wall, above our mapped-out attack, was a hand-painted banner with the words: "WAR ROOM." The message was clear to everyone that entered the room: the Braun family had declared war.

Our life together changed from one of comfortable routines to notifying family, scrambling to find the best oncologists and surgeons, making appointments and arranging travel.

Periodically we would grow quiet, figuratively coming up for air, just to make sure neither of us was emotionally spinning out of control.

The life we had known was stopped in its tracks.

Long before George's cancer entered our home and stopped our life cold, I had already learned what it felt like to be stopped. My life has been earmarked by moments that brought everything to a halt.

These moments forced me to pause, reassess, and sometimes choose a new direction. Some arrived with devastation, others with unexpected joy. Each one altered the course of my life in ways I could not fully understand at the time.

When I Was Nine or Ten

I remember a news story that scared me and rocked my core. It was a report of a woman trying to run away from an attacker. She was raped and murdered, and no one came to her aid.

Before that broadcast, I had no understanding of sex, rape, murder, or that people would not help someone who was being harmed. My life changed.

Just Before Adulthood: High School

I never expected my high school algebra teacher to inappropriately kiss me. I was not prepared for the life-altering changes that would occur because of the emotions and actions resulting from that singular, momentary kiss.

The Phone Call About Mom

Eight years after my wedding to my former algebra teacher, the state of our marriage was even worse than our finances and the half-finished remodel project of our house. At that point in my life I was trying to figure a way out of the marriage, without admitting to my family that I had made a mistake.

I was in my house, standing at the bottom of an extension ladder that was substituting for stairs leading to the second floor, when my sister Fran called.

As Fran was talking to me, my surroundings melted away. I was only aware of the phone in my hand and hearing the words that our mother had a tumor in her lung.

My existence became solely focused on my mother, her treatment, and her care. It didn't take me long to make the decision to move to the same city as Mom and help my sisters care for her.

The news of my mother's cancer stopped me long enough to evaluate what I was doing and change the direction of my life.

Meeting George

Focusing on my mother's health gave me a chance to envision and create a new life for myself.

About nine months after I moved to be closer to my family, I met George. It was an amazing, event-filled swirl of rapid-fire dates that culminated in our marriage just ten months later.

A Wonderful Phone Call

Years after we were married and following a series of three hurricanes, George and I were up on the roof of our home. We had been working all day replacing and securing shingles, when we received a phone call.

Our adoption lawyer's office called to let us know that a set of birth parents had chosen us to be the adoptive parents of their beautiful, gestating baby girl.

Our hearts soared! We toasted the amazing news of our growing family with tears and cold beers from the rooftop as we watched the sunset that evening.

We were joyfully stopped in our tracks.

* * *

Reflections of Collateral Beauty
As a result of these life-defining events, I survived an unhealthy first marriage and the distance it created between me and my family.

I then divorced that same man, moved closer to home, and re-established family ties.

I met and married the love of my life, adopted my little girl, changed careers, and followed my calling to write this book.

Chapter 3

Change and Choices

What Can We Choose When Life Chooses for Us?

While death may be forced upon us, we still have choices. Those choices may be a change in mental attitude, or something more concrete—but we still have choices.

* * *

Navigating Loss

It can come quietly

It can come naturally

Change

It has a force that demands attention

Loss is not all about the physical

It can be a change in a relationship

By death

By choosing a different path

– EJ Braun

* * *

Journal Entry – May 11, 2018 (Twenty-six days after his death)

Okay, Honey Bunny, who will I be? What will I choose to do? How will I go about making my change?

You made me smile in my dreams last night. I forgot why or what the dreams were about, but I know it was you.

I didn't choose for you to get sick. I didn't choose to be a widow, but I can choose how to move into the next phase of my life. I can choose my attitude; I can choose to be happy.

I don't understand this raw emotion of grief—how it is utterly uncontrollable. So, I am choosing to ride this emotion, feel it, learn from it, embrace it… I know I will emerge stronger; I would just like to know when.

How can I still love you if you are no longer alive?

Random thought: When one of a pair of lovebirds dies, does the other one die as well?

* * *

Looking back, I can see that I wanted to be done with grieving, not realizing grief was now a permanent part of me.

* * *

Change As a Choice

We can draw on our life lessons to help us navigate change and make better informed decisions. My personal example of this is how I applied advice Cindy gave me as I entered fire school. Utilizing her advice helped me to successfully change my career from teaching to firefighting.

Many years later I used that same advice to help me survive the grief of losing my husband.

Changing Careers and Counting to Ten

Organizing my classroom and teaching my students were a joy. But after more than fourteen years of teaching in the public school system, I felt as if I was going crazy.

No matter how good I was, and I was good, at creating an emotionally and physically safe classroom environment for my students, that safety net evaporated soon after they left the school grounds. I realized my actions had limited impact on my students' home lives.

Knowing this became almost unbearable to me. I was finding it increasingly difficult to leave my work at work.

I am not a complainer, however, when I compared my emotional state at the end of my workday to George's, there was a big difference. Most days I observed my husband come home from a twenty-four-hour shift with a smile on his handsome face, a skip in his step…just happy. I was both intrigued and jealous.

We talked about the future of my career. I was athletic, loved to be outside, worked hard, and enjoyed helping people. Our discussions led us to the conclusion that I should leave teaching and go into firefighting. It felt like a natural and slightly exotic choice. It was a choice that excited me.

But, the only way our family could afford for me to change careers was for me to secure an uncertified position. As an uncertified firefighter, the fire department would cover my tuition for fire school and pay me a salary while I was in school. Double bonus.

It was July 2002. Our city's fire department was accepting applications for uncertified firefighters for the first time in a very long time.

Landing one of those positions was a formidable process. There were strict physical testing requirements, a written exam, a psychological profile, and a final interview.

It wasn't easy, but with the help and support of my family, I secured one of the eight coveted uncertified positions out of more than 400 applicants.

The timing was perfect. I would be able to complete my 2001-2002 teaching contract without interrupting my students' education. Psychologically, this made my transition to firefighting easier.

It felt as if the universe was aligning all of the stars in my favor.

In the fall of 2002, I was thirty-nine years old and about to enter fire college. Physically, I was prepared, and the firefighters in my family (my sister Cindy, her wife

JoAnne, and my husband George) were helping me to mentally prepare.

Firefighter training school (fire college) is a paramilitary environment. Similar to military basic training, the intent is to dismantle false confidence, teach essential skills, and then test those skills under pressure in simulated emergency situations.

This process builds real confidence based on a newly developed skill set. The training is both physically and mentally demanding, requiring focus, discipline and perseverance.

Cindy, my big sister and the second female firefighter to be certified in the state of Florida, gave me invaluable and hard-earned advice. She may have a different opinion, but I did listen to and apply her advice…most of the time.

One of the most important pieces of Cindy's advice was: "Betty Jean, you can do anything for ten seconds." She explained, "It's going to get rough, hot, physically and mentally brutal. You're going to feel as if you can't continue any longer. When you reach that point, just count to ten. If you're still not done, count to ten again. Keep counting to ten until you're done. You can do *anything* for ten seconds."

I applied that advice many times throughout my twelve long weeks of fire college. As I counted to ten, exhausted, vomiting, and willing myself to keep going, I kept reminding myself: "I can do anything for ten seconds."

Successfully completing fire college, I transformed my career path from teaching to firefighting.

I made a choice to change.

Chapter 4

Forced Changes

Not all changes are chosen. Some arrive like an earthquake, unexpected, unpredictable, and leaving us with no alternative.

Primarily, I am calm in emergency situations. I know how to deal with life-and-death emergencies and mitigate crises very well. Cindy often says our chaotic childhood trained us to be good crisis managers.

Before achieving my rank of fire captain, I was a fire lieutenant for several years. As a lieutenant, I was responsible for the well-being of my crew and the fire station.

Before and during George's cancer treatment, I believed I was prepared to handle the ups and downs of life. However, when George died, I found myself at a serious emotional crossroads. How was I going to live without my "Laundry Man"?

* * *

Aside: My Laundry Man
George washed and folded about 86.3 percent of the laundry in our home. He enjoyed *being* "Laundry Man." In fact, one Halloween, he donned a cape made from an old bedsheet, fastened around his neck with a clothespin, and a mask made from dryer sheets–winning "Most Original" that year at the family party.

* * *

As George's cancer progressed, I didn't think about a future without him. I couldn't.

To look at a future without him was admitting all of our efforts, decisions, and the treatments he endured had failed. Those thoughts would bring unimaginable pain.

Death *made* me look.

Deeply grieving, I began to understand that George's death also meant the death of the life I knew.

Change was forced upon me by death.

* * *

Journal Entry – April 21, 2018 (Six days after his death)

I have always embraced change, but I never thought you would really die.

I truly thought you would go into remission, and we would have many more years to bother each other.

I am so sorry.

*It was heartbreaking to see you suffer, but when you died…
I felt as if my soul was pulled from my body.*

*I guess I am panicking a bit; you are no longer here for me
to rely on… Thank you for giving me as much of you as you
did. Thank you.*

* * *

Who was going to teach our thirteen-year-old daughter
all of the lessons a father teaches his daughter?

Who was I going to tell my deepest fears to and share my
personal successes with?

Who would hold me at night as I giggled, cried, or con-
templated life?

How was I going to take care of the house, the dog, the
cats, and keep our family life going… without him? He
was part of me.

His existence in my life made me feel whole. He was the
missing piece that made my life complete, and now he is
gone.

* * *

Journal Entry – April 22, 2018 (Seven days after his death)

*Tonight, I do not wish to cry. Please know, Honey Bunny, I
love you. I miss you, and our lives are forever changed—first
because you were part of us, and it changed again when you
died.*

* * *

When I wrote that, I was equating "not crying" with not honoring George's memory. But I was exhausted. It felt like I was crying all the time and I just needed a break.

* * *

Death instantly changes almost every aspect of life and one's perspective. Instead of being "stopped in my tracks," I felt totally derailed. I also found myself wanting to be where George was and wanting to be present with my daughter.

What followed was not something I expected, but something that crept into my world and commanded my full attention.

Did suicide ever cross my mind? Yes.

* * *

Lifeline Notice:
If you are remotely considering suicide, please set this book aside and reach out for help. At the end of this chapter, I have listed a few national hotlines to call for help. Call a friend, call your therapist, call 9-1-1... just call.

* * *

I began to contemplate my own death. The idea felt disturbingly comforting. If I died, I would not have to face my grief and possibly be able to reunite with my Honey Bunny on "the other side."

These were strange and frighteningly calming thoughts.

Through this abyss of dark thoughts, I heard a voice in my mind. It told me to look ahead, look through my veil of grief and find an opening.

When I took a deep breath and searched for an opening, I envisioned my youngest daughter finding me after my imagined suicide. I was able to feel her grief and pain. Once I saw Emma's grief, I was able to imagine my funeral with my family and friends in attendance.

This was the point at which I realized I did not want to add more sadness to the lives of the people I loved. I also felt there was more I could, needed, and wanted to do in this life.

Then I heard the whisper of Cindy's advice: "Just keep counting to ten, Betty Jean. You can do anything for ten seconds."

I made the choice to live and embrace the changes in my life that death forced upon me.

Breathe and count to ten.

Resources

Suicide & Crisis Support

United States—988 (Call or text)

Canada—988 (Call or text)

UK & Ireland – Samaritans 116 123

Australia Lifeline—13 11 14

International—findahelpline.com to locate crisis support services in your country.

Information was accurate at the time of publication. Readers are encouraged to consult local directories for the most current resources available in their area.

Chapter 5

The First and the Last Times I Lost Him

The First Time I Lost Him
In August 2016, George and I traveled to New York City for his neck dissection.

His surgery began at 9 a.m. After taking my phone number, the surgical nurse promised to keep me informed. The surgery was scheduled to take anywhere from four to six hours.

In reality, George's neck dissection took eleven and a half hours.

At the five-hour mark, the surgical nurse emerged from the operating room, in person, to let me know George was fine. She explained the surgery was more intricate than expected.

I didn't realize her words really meant the cancer was more extensive than expected.

Even without that understanding, I was fearful of what was happening to George, and, as the nurse turned to re-enter the operating room, I reached for my phone to call my best friend.

My breath caught in my throat, and my heart broke as I held my phone.

I could not call my best friend–he was in surgery.

Silently, I began to sob.

I had been stopped in my tracks, again.

* * *

Journal Entry – August, 2018 (Four months after his death)

George and I were a great team. We felt as if we could get through any life event if we worked together. The night of his surgery, when my world stopped for a second, I realized I needed to ask for help. My life partner needed help… and that meant I also needed help.

* * *

Looking back, I can see that my family knew I was in need of help. The night of George's surgery, my cousin, Tracy, drove into New York City from New Jersey to stay with me until my sister, Lori, flew in from Atlanta the next day.

* * *

"Tomorrow is not promised."

— a frequent saying of my friend, Herve Thomas.

* * *

The Last Time I Lost Him-The Final Two Days of George's Life

George and I ran toward live our life together until we were stopped in our tracks one last time.

I am a retired firefighter and paramedic with almost twenty-two years of service.

Approximately eighty percent of all emergency 9-1-1 calls are medical calls. I have witnessed death before, during, and after the soul departs from the physical body. Many times. First responders witness a lot of death.

George's physical death was not all that different from the multitude of deaths I had witnessed in the field. With one exception: George was part of my heart and soul.

On April 14, 2018, the night before George died, we had our immediate family over for a hamburger dinner. George did not eat, but he made the effort to get out of bed and sit in his favorite place on the living room couch.

He had his eyes closed, sitting upright with his chin slightly raised. He was on home oxygen at this point.

When a family member walked into the room, George would open his eyes and slightly smile to let them know he was happy to see them.

He sat there, not moving, for more than six hours.

George then looked at me and said that he wanted to go to bed. He tried to get up on his own but could not. He repeated that he was tired—very tired—and he leaned to his right side and laid his head on the couch. He was in a physically awkward position. He did not look comfortable, nor did he want to be touched.

George removed the oxygen tubing from his face and started to rhythmically breathe.

That was when I knew.

While over the last several months there had been many physical indications and emotional markers to let me know… it was this dinner, this event, this point in time, that I realized George was actively dying.

You would think that when a person connects the dots, there would be some sort of epiphany.

Not for me, not yet.

I was still in work mode.

I enlisted my support team to call my children and bring them home. Lexi was at a wedding in another city; Bailey was at her home in Chicago, and Emma was at Cindy and JoAnne's house with her cousins.

Lexi left the wedding and made her way to her father's side. Bailey spoke with George over the telephone; they cried together. Emma dutifully came back to the house with her Aunt JoAnne.

Emma asked to speak with me in private.

With her eyes filled with tears and not wanting to do anything anyone considered "wrong," she said to me: "Momma, I love Daddy, but I don't want to be here when he dies."

Inside, I felt two emotions: heartbreak for putting Emma in this situation at age 13 and pride in that she was able to tell me what was in her heart.

JoAnne took Emma Jean back to her home to be with her cousins.

From 8 p.m. until about 10 p.m., George was in, what I thought to be, a very uncomfortable position, rhythmically breathing, not wanting to be touched, and his eyes were closed.

I gently, quietly, and calmly pleaded with George to allow me to make him more comfortable. I explained that I would get help to lift him up and get him to our bedroom.

He politely agreed.

He never spoke again.

Once George was in our bedroom and able to lie down, we used pillows to prop him up on his left side, as it seemed easier for him to breathe in that position.

We gave him the hospice prescribed doses of morphine to help with pain and ease his breathing.

George wanted only a few people around him as he was dying.

Weeks earlier, we had talked about his wishes during and after his death.

As we–his eldest daughter, my oldest sister, and a few other caregivers, and I–kept vigil to meet his needs, I prayed for God to help my husband die quickly and peacefully.

George made it through the night, and we all took turns seeing to his needs.

During the evening of April 15th, when we all knew the end was near, Cindy asked me a question. "Would you like to be alone with George?"

I was afraid to say yes.

This was the moment in my life that I knew he was going to die. My husband was going to die soon. And although I prayed for his quick and painless death, I did not want it to happen.

My answer to Cindy's question was "No."

I thank the Lord every time I think of that night and that Cindy did not accept my "no." Somehow, she *knew* I needed to be alone with my husband.

My sister gently gathered Lexi; they said their final good-byes to George and quietly left the room.

Surprising feelings came over me when the door silently closed behind them. I did not feel the need to be strong for Lexi, or to consider anyone's feelings, except for my own.

I felt afraid. I was going to be the only one in the room when George died. But I also felt free to *feel* everything.

Alone with my dying husband, that is when our life together seemed to play like a movie before my eyes. I knew he was slipping away.

Feeling a strong sense of urgency to speak, I did.

I spoke of how much I loved our life together and how grateful I was that he allowed me to be myself.

The team we created by being a family was magical, and I thanked him for our child. I promised to take care of her.

I thanked him for the honor of being allowed to get to know his other two children.

I thanked him for being such a good father, husband, and friend, and told him that I was so sorry cancer had happened to him.

I loved him; I told him over and over again.

I was the only one to observe George's last breaths, during which I apologized for everything I could remember.

As George breathed for the very last time, an animalistic, guttural cry surged from my body, and I felt as if my heart and soul were being fractured and torn apart.

* * *

George, my Honey Bunny, died in my arms at 8 p.m. on April 15, 2018.

* * *

Chapter 6

The Quiet That Followed

In death, his body was finally able to relax.

The surgical scar on his neck no longer contorted his face. He looked like the handsome man I had always known, and I am so grateful for that final vision.

We washed his hair and dressed him in his favorite Hawaiian shirt and comfortable shorts. He was at peace.

* * *

Journal Entry – Undated pages 2021 (Three years after his death)

I don't understand what is happening. Is the soul actually torn, or is it only missing a piece… a person?

* * *

Journal Entry– December 2021 (Three and a half years after his death)

Does the torn soul ever heal, or does life simply weave its fabric enough to hold it together until peace and death are achieved?

* * *

Excerpt from my memorial words at George's Celebration of Life:

"Our intertwined lives were filled with love, respect, and belief in each other. Thank you, Honey Bunny, I love you."

* * *

When the celebration of life ended and co-workers, friends, and family went home, I was left to figure out my new life.

And as much as my family loved me and tried to help me every step of the way, this was something I had to face… on my own.

* * *

Count to ten. Look for bubbles… they will lead you up.

Chapter 7

Collateral Change

Learning to Expect the Unexpected: Holidays, Identity, and Long-Term Grief

Living As Newly Widowed
George's illness and death brought my family and friends closer and into my immediate circle of life. But I also felt the full and utter solitude of being alone.

I was alone… but surrounded by love.

Count to ten.

Returning to Life After Loss
Weeks after George's death, I went back to work, Emma went back to school, and we slowly plowed through life.

Examining my "new life," I felt the excruciating pain of death. This pain was not only for the loss of my husband but also for the loss of the life I had known for over 23 years. Seven months after George died, the veil of grief and loss remained thick around me. I was attentively journaling my experiences and emotions. What I experienced next, however, was unexpected.

The holidays became my first real glimpse of who I was becoming after losing George. The first major family holiday arrived: Thanksgiving. I had more than twenty-three years of a wonderful marriage. I had my health, my children, my home, and my firefighting career. Was I thankful? Yes, I was thankful.

My focus was to keep some kind of continuity for the children around the holidays. Even so, I proposed Thanksgiving pizza as a new holiday tradition. The proposal was met with quiet stares and side glances that made me think an alien had invaded my body.

Losing the Holiday Feeling
I used to be the person who energetically embraced each holiday. Often, I was warmly teased by my family for my themes and crafts. Handcrafting Thanksgiving hats, embroidering turkeys on napkins and stitching images of Santa Claus on kitchen towels are a few examples.

My last great adventure of crafting for the family was for our 2016 family trip. One of my nieces organized a family Christmas-New Year's Day holiday getaway to Lake Tahoe, Nevada, and many of our family members jumped on board.

Planning began in the spring of 2016, before George was diagnosed with cancer.

Once he was diagnosed and a treatment plan was set, we decided to honor our commitment to travel with the family. Lake Tahoe for Christmas and New Year's…something enjoyable and fun to look forward to.

George's surgery, chemotherapy, and radiation would be completed by early November, 2016. George would have six weeks to recover before the trip.

I decided, because I was spending many hours in waiting rooms to support George, that I would keep busy by knitting winter hats for the family. Using a circular loom, I knitted twenty winter hats.

So, yes, I was that person. But after losing George, suddenly I wasn't.

I knew I was changing; I could feel it, but I couldn't understand why I was changing. My desire for large family gatherings evaporated along with my desire for crafty, creative themes.

I felt a lot of guilt.

A Shift That Wasn't Temporary
At first, I chalked this change up to a temporary situation brought on by the recent loss of my husband, as well as the loss of my mother, who died four months before him.

After the first year of holidays passed, I expected a flood of emotion along with my desire to celebrate each holiday to return.

Year two of the holidays came and went. Nothing.

Year three–nope.

Year four, I eliminated most of my holiday decorations, not wanting to expend the energy to decorate.

So, as it turned out, this was not a temporary situation. This was not a phase. I am no longer the person who enjoys making Christmas tree decorations for the entire extended family.

While I still enjoy the memories of past holidays and understand why the celebrations take place, I no longer want to be an intricate part of them.

I would rather be in a hot tub with a glass of champagne, snowflakes gently falling, with the mountains of Telluride, Colorado as my backdrop.

The idea of cool quiet air blanketing my body and mind is soothing to my soul.

Still, feeling a little broken about this part of my life, I began to examine my feelings more intently.

* * *

"If all you can do is crawl, then crawl."

–Rumi

* * *

Change is inevitable. We can be a part of the process or feel as if it has been forced on us. In reality, it may be a little of both. There should be no judgment.

I was feeling judged, mostly by myself.

* * *

Journal Entry – January 2025 (Seven years after his death)

The holidays are done… I think I need to come to terms with how I feel about them…just like I come to terms with other events I cannot control…I can enjoy the season of summer turning into fall with the beauty of the changing leaves, or rail against it and the mess the falling leaves make.

* * *

Learning From Change
Sometimes change brings comfort. Other times, change brings pain. In my sixty-plus years on this earth, I can say that change has always brought me growth.

The overwhelming nature of change can make your head spin and blur your focus on life, making it impossible to know what to do next.

I was taught, as many of us were, while learning to swim in the ocean, that if you get tossed around or pulled under, look for the bubbles–look for the light.

If you follow the bubbles to the light, they will lead you to the surface; they will help you find your way out.

I turned this advice into imagery in my meditation, and it has helped guide me.

* * *

Turbulent Survival

As you tumble in the turbulent water of grief

As you struggle for air to breathe

Relax

Let your body move

Look for light

Swim to the bubbles

Count to ten

–EJ Braun

* * *

Chapter 8

A Missing Roadmap of Life: Loving After Death

Finding the Rhythm of Your Changed Life

I've decided to live…now what?

Nothing had I lived through prepared me for these life chapters: the chapter of George getting sick and the realization that he was going to die; the chapter of surviving his death and choosing to live through the pain of grief; the chapter that required me to continue our family without him; the chapter of living through our daughter's "firsts" without him; and the chapter of realizing I was now a single parent.

But most of all, there was the chapter of understanding that death was not the end of my relationship with my husband.

You Should Be Here

The wonderful, magical moments

That should be shared with you

Are lost in the tears streaming down my face

Happy moments in time…

Her first car

Drawing on her arm with permanent marker

Starting college

I wanted to share all of them with you

Where are you?

Why did you go?

I want you back

I am drowning and feel so lonely.
—EJ Braun

* * *

After Honey Bunny's death, I continued to talk to him. At the end of each day, I told him what he had missed and how it felt without him.

The following excerpts from my journal show how, even though someone is dead, they remain alive–in our hearts and emotions–and an integral part of our lives.

The journal entries I have chosen will also give the reader a glimpse into the rhythm of feelings and the tempo of healing that occurs during grief.

You do not need to understand everything here. I didn't.

You are not alone.

* * *

Journal Entry – April 26, 2018 (Eleven days after his death)

Honey, I know we constantly told each other and acknowledged that together we made a great team.

Yesterday, I felt so weak without you.

We were each other's ballast, and I feel so lost and afraid that I am going to lose my footing and not be able to do anything.

Cindy made a wonderful meatloaf.

I was not promoted to District Chief, and now I am going to bed.

* * *

Journal Entry – April 27, 2018 (Twelve days after his death)

I woke up and, for just a minute, forgot that you had died.

Those few seconds were euphoric, carefree.

Reality crashed my party, and my euphoria was crushed under the weight of grief… but I think a bit of it splattered up and remains, because you are no longer suffering.

No pain.

I am so mad that you had to go through all of that.

I am mad at the universe, yet grateful you no longer suffer.

* * *

Journal Entry – April 29, 2018 (Funeral Day – Pre-Funeral)

I woke up not wanting to wake up unless your cancer and death were just a dream.

But the chickens just wouldn't stop clucking, so I got up.

Soon the house was filled with the sounds of life. Our family, our friend Herve, his wife, and daughter were here to have a toast to you, my love, at 10:16 a.m., in honor of our marriage (Our wedding day was 10:16 a.m. on October 16, 1994).

The countdown is on. Only a few hours until your funeral, and then your life celebration will only be a memory but forever seared into my brain along with your love, which will last forever in my heart.

* * *

Journal Entry – April 29, 2018 (Funeral Day – Post-Funeral)

You were honored today—not only by me but by the fire service, and not just for your specific contributions but for your ethics, dedication, and personal convictions.

I wanted so much to see your face and feel the squeeze of your hand on my shoulder.

I know in my head you are gone, but I still don't want to believe it.

I want you to walk through the door saying, "Hello, Hellooooo, Helloooooooooooo," to the point I am irritated.

I know that will never happen again.

How can it be that you are gone, and yet it feels like you are here?

How can it be that I love you so much, yet you are dead?

* * *

Journal Entry – May 1, 2018 (Sixteen days after his death)

I woke up with no sorrow—as if you had not been sick, as if you had not died.

That did not last long.

It is you in whom I want to confide; it is you that I trusted.

We were "one." You died… so logic says I also must have died.

How is my heart still beating?

The kids broke the fence.

* * *

Journal Entry – May 3, 2018 (Eighteen days after his death)

This grieving is for the birds.

We were not perfect together, but we were really good and embraced each other.

The world keeps moving. I feel like I am wearing cement boots.

* * *

Journal Entry – May 8, 2018 (Twenty-three days after his death)

Today seemed almost normal, but then the sadness broke through, and the tears began to flow, as if someone turned on the faucet in my eyes.

* * *

Journal Entry – May 9, 2018 (Twenty-four days after his death)

I am worried I will be alone as I get older, but I cannot help that right now.

I think I need to just grieve, live life, relish the memories I have of me and George together, and focus on Emma's healing.

* * *

Journal Entry – May 10, 2018 (Twenty-five days after his death)

Last night, I dreamt you were laughing and giving me little nuggets of advice.

I awoke feeling relaxed, happy, and full.

I miss you.

I am not ready to be the new me. I liked the me with you just fine.

Logic tells me I need to move on, but I can't rush this. I think I am really supposed to feel this.

* * *

Journal Entry – May 12, 2018 (Twenty-seven days after his death)

No more arguments, no more banter, no more knowing looks, no more trying to figure out how to save your life.

It's all over but the pain of letting you go and knowing you are now only a memory.

* * *

Journal Entry – May 13, 2018 – Mother's Day (Twenty-eight days after his death)

This morning, I awoke talking to you, reaffirming your death and reliving the many Mother's Days you helped create.

So many wonderful memories… In the morning, a card leaning against a vase of beautiful fresh flowers, and a gentle hug always accompanied your affirmation that you were certain I was a wonderful mother.

I have these memories to cherish for the rest of my life.

* * *

Journal Entry – May 14, 2018 – Return to Work (Twenty-nine days after his death)

George, my Honey Bunny… I miss your belief in me.

You are woven into every single memory of my firefighting career.

In my most difficult moments, I reached for you to share my worries and concerns. I have no one now.

Thank you for being my go-to for so long.

* * *

As I look back on my journal entries, I can see that I am sometimes speaking directly to George, sometimes I am just placing my thoughts on paper, and other times I speak to him, and then the universe in the same journal entry.

What I was feeling created a rhythm in my heart and mind. There was the slow and tentative rhythm of building gratitude that was interrupted by the violent and disjointed rhythm of anger and anguish.

In the days that followed, my journal became a place where anger, gratitude, confusion, and longing collided without warning.

* * *

Journal Entry – May 16, 2018 (Thirty-one days after his death)

Going back to work is good for me; however, when I get home, I don't know what to do. I will give myself time and space to come up with a plan.

I still don't know how to master living with only the memory of you.

I miss our morning coffee and our afternoon cocktails together.

* * *

Journal Entry – May 17, 2018 (Thirty-two days after his death)

I keep expecting you and Toby to be here… 'Great Expectations.' Rest well and know that I know I will be okay. I also know it is going to take some time.

Toby was our eleven-year-old black Labrador-Chow mix dog. He died suddenly two nights before George's funeral.

* * *

Journal Entry – May 20, 2018 (Thirty-five days after his death)

I woke up early. I didn't wake up afraid or lonely… I just woke up.

I know my grief will return, but right now, I feel pretty good. I miss the hell out of you.

You would have loved today on the back porch swing—the birds, the quiet, the temperature, the coffee.

What I miss most is you.

* * *

When George was in the hospital, I bought him a small magnet with these words. We spoke about them often:

"Life isn't about waiting for the storm to pass

It's about learning to dance in the rain."

–Vivian Greene

* * *

A Forced Change in the Relationship
I found it ironic that death was forcing me to let go of my emotional attachment to my husband.

We had worked for years to develop and hone our mutual attachment to each other in order to become a team. Now I was supposed to let that attachment evaporate the moment he died.

This realization pretty much pissed me off.

* * *

I wish someone had given me the memo.

* * *

Journal Entry – September 2021 (Three years after his death)

This morning, an online post prompted me–jogged my memory–to play Elton John's song 'Can You Feel the Love Tonight,' our wedding song.

I rose from bed, crossed my hands over my heart, swayed in rhythm, and cried out for my lost half. I spoke to him and felt a sense of comfort as my tears freely fell.

The memory of George– his scent, and the lost feeling of completeness…

* * *

Maintaining Love While Creating a New Life
There was, and continues to be, a lot of emotional work to do in order to let my love for George transform.

It is my desire to maintain his memory and significance for his children–and for my own mental well-being.

Sometimes, it seems it would be so much easier to clear the house and my mind of all aspects of this human and never speak of him again.

The blaring reality is that I cherish George. I still love him. I love our memories, and I do not want to erase him from my life.

The difficulty is striking the balance between honoring my love for George and creating a healthy new life for myself.

Chapter 9

Finding the Rhythm

Music has always had a strong presence in my life.

My early years, in Harris Hill Elementary School, I sang in the chorus (I even played Ebenezer Scrooge in *The Christmas Carol* for my fifth-grade pageant) and later, my violin lessons in Penfield Junior High School taught me how to read music.

By no means am I an accomplished musician; I play music for my own enjoyment.

I have always found it intriguing that the same musical notes can evoke entirely different feelings. Played one way, a song may feel light and upbeat. But if you change the tempo, the strength of the notes, or the timing, the very same song can feel sad or angry.

The rhythm of grief is *not* like the predictable rhythm of music. Like the rhythm of a song, grief moves fluidly, but predictability is not appreciated or felt until the exact rhythm is understood. Grief is not easy to understand or anticipate, because it changes as it moves through you.

The closest I can come to describing the rhythm of grief is comparing it to *learning* to play a difficult song on the guitar.

That sounds simplistic.

Let me explain this metaphor further.

I begin at the start of the song with the first three chords. I strum each of the three chords to make sure my fingers know where to go.

Then I play the chords in the order they appear in the first phrase of the song.

Next, I play those chords in the rhythm of the song.

Then I add the words.

I repeat this process until I can play the music and sing the words at the same time.

Once I can play that portion of the song well enough to recognize the tune, I move on to the next phrase and repeat the process.

As I transition from the first to the second phrase, my timing and finger placement falter until my body and brain coordinate their efforts.

I work on the song in this manner until I can play it in its entirety. Even after I feel I have mastered a song, it can still give me unexpected problems.

A string may break, or I may have a moment when my mind blanks and I forget the sequence of chords–or the words that go with them.

Other days, I can play and sing the song with ease and very few mistakes.

For me, that is the rhythm of grief.

You heal a part of your mind, or heart, or soul, and then grief moves to a different part of your life that needs attention.

Then you have to figure out how to navigate the next part.

Sometimes grief requires you to revisit something you thought you had already come to terms with.

Past experiences with death, trauma, the quality of a relationship that ended, and many other factors all figure into the formation of this unique rhythm.

It is critical to recognize the signs so that each person can give themselves permission to honor and ride the rhythmic waves of grief.

Just as the energy of the magnificent ocean cannot be stopped, we cannot stop the waves of grief.

We can, however, count to ten, look for the bubbles that will lead us to the surface, and give ourselves time to breathe as we learn the newest facet of grief that presents itself in our own unique rhythm.

* * *

Journal Entry – March 2021 (Three years after his death)

This wave of grief has passed. The water feels calm, and my breath is easy.

* * *

Journal Entry – May 2, 2019 (One year after his death)

These last few months have been emotionally difficult. To keep alive the family traditions, I forced myself to decorate for each holiday: Halloween, Thanksgiving, Christmas, Valentine's Day, St. Patrick's Day, and Easter.

Each time I pulled out the decorations, a flood of memories of you and how we would pick out presents, and decorate, and banter back and forth until we both would laugh or get slightly annoyed…

And while at times it seemed like I was just going through the motions of decorating, inside, I really wanted to want to decorate…to enjoy the holidays…There were parts that I truly enjoyed, but then, in the quiet of my mind, I felt your absence and the feelings of my loss seemed to be getting more acute instead of easing up.

My final straw was April 15th, one year since your death. My heart seemed so raw all over again, and I continuously cried.

* * *

Journal Entry – May 19, 2019 (One year after his death)

I refuse to feel broken. I am strong. I can feel my energy building. I want to dance. I want to laugh. I want to be held. I feel this energy wanting to burst out of me, as if I am just getting started.

* * *

When Grief Catches You Off Guard

My rhythm of grief has the inconvenient theme of catching me off guard when I am least expecting to be brought down to my emotional knees.

* * *

Journal Entry – May 2019 (One year after his death)

My bed, our bed, our life, dreams, and plans all skip like a scratched record and play over in my mind.

White noise is what I hear as I wake up, as my mind clears from sleep. Reality comes into focus as I make the bed, fluff my pillow, and ready myself for the day.

* * *

Dream State of Grief

I turn over and reach....

For nothing... for everything

My fingers feel only the cold sheets, where you should be

No warmth, no comfort...your head no longer on your
pillow

Nothing but... gone

My heart

The life we built

Gone

Empty

–EJ Braun

Chapter 10

Coffin, Urn, or Both?

Waves of Grief and Humor
To give you a sense of my thought process and how the waves of grief began, this chapter will take you from the day following George's death through his funeral.

I insert humor because humor, love, and wonderful memories have helped me to survive.

My journal entries capture my immediate emotions and thoughts as I worked to find the rhythm of my grief.

Funeral Preparations
Have you ever purchased, and then sold a coffin?

Before I tell this story, there is some information you need to know.

In the days surrounding my Honey Bunny's death, I was busy making funeral plans. Of course, George and I had discussed his wishes prior to his death, and I had already met with the funeral director to make official arrangements.

Even though many of the arrangements were made, plenty of decisions remained after George's death. I distinctly remember sitting on the living room floor in my long-sleeved, blue-and-white checkered cotton pajamas, figuring out what items would be needed for the funeral.

The computer screen was displayed on the TV, and I was using a wireless keyboard.

My loving and ever-present support team was with me. I know I had support because with each online purchase I shared pictures, and we shared our emotions—first, laughter, because we couldn't believe the variety of funeral items available or that we could buy this shit online.

Signs, urns, "suggestions," family packs of urns, memory blankets… anything a grieving person could imagine or desire—everything except a working spell to bring back your loved one whole and healthy.

I checked for that, too.

After the laughter came tears, because reality was slowly setting in, and we couldn't believe George was actually gone.

Understand, my support team and I were present when George's body physically died. I was there to see him take his very last breath. It continues to confound me how disbelief can exist even after witnessing such an event.

Finally, more laughter, because we knew that George would have been "all in" with making these purchases.

In life, George was a natural-born shopper, deal finder, and thoughtful gift-giver.

Purchasing the Urn
I first purchased an urn from an online resource.

It was, and remains, a beautiful fourteen-inch-tall cut-glass urn, with an opaque, silverish-gray background.

The design features nine large cut-glass tulips. The tulip stems begin at the base and expand into the petals about two-thirds of the way up the urn. Each flower has two leaves, and each leaf touches the leaf of the flower on either side.

It was beautiful online and stunning in person.

My original thought was, "I can purchase an urn online for a lot less than what the funeral home will charge."

This statement was, and remains, true. I *could* have purchased an urn for about one-third of the price that the funeral home was going to charge. Is that what I did?

No.

I, under no pressure from any outside source, purchased this beautiful urn, knowing that George would have loved this contemporary yet classic design. The cost, while not astronomical, was higher than anything I was looking at during my planning sessions at the funeral home.

I understand the irony.

The satisfaction of knowing that my Honey Bunny is being honored in this beautiful memorial vessel is priceless.

The Coffin
As I thought about the "event" of George's funeral, I envisioned the attendees, how the venue would be staged, the slideshow set to music that included photos from all facets of George's life, his portrait on display, and his ashes.

His ashes, in this beautiful urn, would appear so small compared to the giant of a personality that we all knew and loved so dearly.

I opened my laptop and declared, "Honey Bunny needs a coffin!"

The members of my support team—I remember the looks—were stunned. They were stunned because George, after all, was cremated.

One does not normally need a coffin for ashes. I was aware of this. But I wanted him to be carried into the church by the Fire Department. It would have looked pretty silly: eight uniformed firefighters carrying one fourteen-inch cut-glass urn etched with tulips.

So, I opted for the additional purchase of a coffin. I realize how odd it may seem to buy a coffin to carry an urn.

To tell you the truth, I have been told I am odd–but in a cute way.

Being somewhat of a tree-hugging, environmentally conscious person, I purchased a beautiful, plain, and simple pinewood coffin kit that I could assemble.

My support team, at this point, was starting to ask pertinent questions to determine my mental stability. Questions were tossed out like… "Impulse purchase?" "Are you sure?" "Where are you going to store it?" and "Do you know who the president is?"

All good questions, and my responses were stellar.

Impulse? George is dead; I don't really have time to wait for a sale.

Was I sure? Well, not really… but the cost was not going to break the bank.

Purchasing a coffin in addition to an urn was not an action equivalent to planning on quitting my job, joining a circus, and learning to be a trapeze artist–although, as the funeral date got closer and rapid-fire decisions were required, the thought of running away to join the circus briefly crossed my mind.

As far as storing the coffin after the funeral, I have a big shed, no problem.

The last question my support team posed, about the name of the president, I verbally ignored, because they were just being downright obnoxious. As I was confident they were interjecting first responder humor, my response was a brief, but well-understood, hand gesture.

I hit "enter" on my computer, and the coffin was ordered.

Have you ever second-guessed a purchase?

I am stubborn, but I woke up the next day and said to myself, "What in the hell did I do?" So, I decided to swallow my pride and call the coffin company to cancel my order.

The phone call went something like this: "Hello, I would like to cancel my coffin purchase from yesterday evening."

The very solemn, yet compassionate, voice on the other end extended his sincere condolences for my loss and slowly explained that shipping had already occurred because, when people place an order such as this–meaning a coffin–they need the item rather quickly.

My coffin would arrive in two days.

Assembling a Coffin
What was I to do? The only thing a widow could do at this point: convene a coffin-assembling event in the driveway of my home.

The coffin was assembled by a core group of family and friends. We set up a shade tent, made mimosas, Bloody Marys, Sprite for the kids, and munched on snacks.

George was on everyone's mind.

I could not concentrate enough to follow the directions for assembling the coffin, so my friends and family took over. I mostly watched and facilitated the eating and drinking.

Everyone made sure to have a part in the assembly, even if it meant only placing one screw in one board.

The completely assembled coffin was beautiful. It was made from quality wood and assembled with utter love.

* * *

Journal Entry – April 21, 2018 – Building the coffin (Six days after his death)

Today I did not want to wake up. My arms and legs feel like lead. Instead of getting better, I am missing you more.

I set up a party to build your casket. I am uncertain whether you would like it or hate it, it's all I know how to do.

We had a good time… but I am beside myself. I just want to scream, and I don't know what to do.

Tomorrow is Sunday. It will be seven days already that you are gone.

* * *

A Gift of Shared Grief: More Collateral Beauty
Sometimes the worst moments in life can bring a sense of fulfillment. Who would think that building a coffin for my deceased husband would bring fond memories to my consciousness?

Life is amazing.

As you might imagine, we laughed at the seeming absurdity of assembling a coffin in my driveway. Stories of George were freely shared, we cried, laughed some more, and hugged.

The initial, absurd, yet well-intentioned impulse buy from the internet brought some peace and laughter to my house of mourning.

At the end of the event, my broken heart felt some warmth.

That was a miracle.

*　*　*

Excerpt from Lexi's memorial words at George's Celebration of Life:

"He didn't wait to love us; he didn't wait to celebrate. And even now, without him, we don't wait to celebrate him or to turn a dark moment into a casket-building party. It looks great, by the way."

*　*　*

"Live in each moment; feel each tiny miracle."

– EJ Braun

* * *

Selling the Coffin–Years Later
Five and a half years later grief surprised me again, this time in my shed. The coffin had been dismantled and wrapped to preserve it from Florida insects (cockroaches), and as planned, stored in my shed.

Through the years, I have read a few books, articles, etc., on decluttering one's life and house. In fact, I am a person who believes in getting rid of "things" that are no longer needed.

One day, I was rearranging a bunch of "crap" I didn't need in my outdoor shed. I spent the day taking pictures and placing unwanted items that were in good shape on a social media selling site.

Yep, I did it.

My thought process went something like this:

"The coffin isn't taking up much space…"

"You don't need this coffin right now…"

"But it was George's coffin!"

"The kids aren't going to use it…"

"I'm not going to use it…"

"And I don't want to turn the coffin into a Halloween decoration."

"What will people think?"

"How much do you even charge for a used coffin?"

"Who is actually going to purchase a used coffin?"

As my mind continued its swirl of questions, my fingers independently created the ad on my phone. Momentarily, my index finger hovered over the "Post" button. I raised my eyebrows, grinned at myself, then published the ad. I placed George's coffin up for sale–but not before I blocked my friends and family from seeing the ad I published on social media.

For some reason, I did not want anyone I knew to be aware that I was selling a coffin, George's coffin.

I have a feeling I know what you may be thinking: "Did someone really buy the coffin?" Yes, someone really bought my Honey Bunny's coffin for their deceased loved one.

I sold a used coffin. There was never an actual body in the coffin; it only contained the ashes of a body in a beautiful, classically designed cut-glass urn. But yeah–I sold a coffin.

I still do not know why that makes me smile at myself. Maybe one day I will understand.

* * *

On a serious note, the couple who purchased my husband's coffin was in desperate need of a coffin for a deceased loved one's quick funeral and burial, owing to religious constraints.

While I continue to laugh at myself for placing an ad to sell a used coffin, my heart is satisfied that George's coffin was able to honorably fill the need of a grieving family.

* * *

Journal Entry – April 18, 2018 (Three days after his death)

I woke up, and you were still not here. Before I open my eyes and before my mind clears from the night, I am happy and think you are still waking up beside me.

It doesn't take long for reality to make itself known, and I realize my life has truly changed forever. I wish we could have lived our lives together longer.

* * *

* * *

He Is Not Dead

"I cannot say, and I will not say
That he is dead. He is just away.

With a cheery smile, and a wave of the hand,
He has wandered into an unknown land

And left us dreaming how very fair
It needs must be, since he lingers there.

And you—oh you, who the wildest yearn
For an old-time step, and the glad return,

Think of him faring on, as dear
In the love of There as the love of Here.

Think of him still as the same. I say,
He is not dead—he is just away."

–James Whitcomb Riley

* * *

Chapter 11

Holding Space for Those Who Are Gone

* * *

In private, this is when I weep

When my heart dares to open

So that I may feel and try to heal

This deep hole—an empty space

A wound

A passage to my last life.

–EJ Braun

* * *

Journal Entry – April 18, 2022 (Four years after his death)

Today is a few days past the four-year anniversary of Honey Bunny's death.

This year was not the dramatic upwelling of pent-up emotive feelings that gushed as I spoke. It was more of a powerful swell that allowed me to wade through with steadfast footing …

Only after the swell passed did my footing give way to bended knee with a kind of controlled release of pain, deep sorrow, and longing.

I was drawn to re-read the tributes that Cindy, Lexi, and I gave to the gathering of people for George's Celebration of Life. I remember I wrote mine late at night by hand. The words effortlessly flowed from my heart onto the paper.

Even as I re-read the words, four years old, my heart surged as it reached toward George, with the pride of our relationship shining as an example of love and unconditional acceptance for another human being.

* * *

What Does "Holding Space" Really Mean?
One piece of advice that I heard from multiple sources encourages those who are bereaved to "hold space" for the grieving process and our lost loved ones.

The idea of holding space sounded valid and was imparted by people I love and trust. But the advice I was getting raised questions in my mind.

How does one hold space for those who are gone from your life? Is it tangible space or emotional space? If it's a physical area or objects, how do you hold that space and make it not weird for visitors? How long do you hold space for a lost loved one? Do you explain the space? What does the space you're holding "do?"

As my Honey Bunny would say to me when he was alive, "You ask so many questions."

I have come to understand that holding space is whatever I want it to be. I can honor my deceased loved ones free from judgment and artificially imposed timelines.

If I want to cover my wall with photos of George, create a shrine, or light a candle for his birthday–that is all considered holding space.

For friends and family who accept my "holding space," it means that they let me hold space for George any way I want to, for as long as I need or desire, minus the judgment.

How the Seed for Dating Was Planted
You may not be ready to even think of dating; it took me over two years for that thought to turn into a plausible desire.

And even if you never date again, which is the case for my first cousin once removed, holding space can seem uncomfortable for those around us.

Barbara Jean, my cousin, lost her husband (Don) ten months before I lost George.

Cindy and I visited our cousin in her home about a year after George died. The visit was pleasant, but what hung in the air for me was our shared bond of recently losing our husbands.

Once we broke the silence, our tears freely fell as we expressed our sympathy for each other's loss.

As Barbara Jean was giving us the tour of her home, I commented on a beautiful shadow box with preserved red roses that hung in her living room. She explained that those were the roses that had been placed on Don's coffin and said "Some people may not like it, but that's just tough."

Barbara Jean further explained that Don's sneakers and slippers were still under his side of the bed and she had no intention of moving them.

She made a wonderful dinner. We caught up on family news and as Cindy and I were getting ready to leave, our cousin planted a seed of wisdom as we were standing in her kitchen.

Barbara Jean told me, in her strong but warm Italian-New Jersey way, "Now me… I am a one-man woman, I'm not interested in another man. I am not interested in dating. Don was it for me. You, Betty Jean… you're young (I was fifty-five years old at that time) you could and should date… but ONLY when you're ready. I can see you're not ready, but you will be."

When I contacted Barbara Jean about permission to use that memory and her name in this book she gave me an update. The family now loves the roses that continue to hang in her living room, Don's sneakers and slippers remain under his side of the bed, all his clothes remain in the dresser and his shower robe hangs in the closet. She finds it difficult to believe that eight and a half years have passed.

It is important to give yourself permission to openly remember and speak of the dead.

But "holding space" can also serve as an opening for those around us who may not know what to say or do with their own grief surrounding your loved one. The opening might allow them to feel comfortable enough to speak of your loved one and to help them process their individual grief.

I call that a "Collateral Grief Blessing."

Examples of How I Openly Hold Space for George
I have a collage of individual pictures of George with me and each of his three children, prominently displayed in my living room. Whoever enters my home undoubtedly will see this tribute to a wonderful husband, father, and friend.

The collage of pictures, to me, sets the tone in our home. He is not gone; he's just away.

Another way I hold space is that I openly talk of George with my friends and family. At first, I would feel the emotions build and tears of loss fall, but I would continue to tell the story and share the memory. "Remember when George would…" or "Do you remember when my Honey Bunny…" I believe this gave my friends and family permission to openly remember him and share their love, loss, and grief.

George also has a dedicated shelf in my music room, a private place where I go for "me time." It holds his ashes, the flag that draped his coffin, my favorite picture of him in his uniform, and an electric candle that serves as an eternal flame in my mind.

A favorite picture of me and George hangs on a wall in my bedroom so that I can see him each morning.

In my closet, I keep a five-inch glass heart with his ashes encased within. A smaller heart hangs from my truck's rearview mirror.

I may have gone overboard getting his ashes encased in glass. I have two glass roosters (one for me and one for Emma), a bud vase for Lexi, and a black and white hummingbird for myself. I also had several yellow-gold blobs that I gave to each of the kids and a few other family members, and an abstract swirl that serves as a sun-catcher.

His many awards and plaques from work are displayed on the wall of a spare bedroom; maybe the kids will one day want those keepsakes.

For me, the experience of openly remembering my lost partner has been liberating and a blessing, not only for me, but also for those around me.

George's Request

The main reason I will always hold space for George is because of a request he made on the day he was placed on hospice care.

Ever gracious, that day he was no different.

Honey Bunny had been poked and prodded, his neck dissected, filled with chemo, zapped with radiation, hospitalized for chemo-induced kidney failure, had his gallbladder removed, suffered a crushed lumbar vertebra, and endured gout in his right big toe.

The list could continue, but you get the idea. He had been through so much in the last twenty months of his life.

When the doctor recommended hospice care, George stated, "I thought it was time." Talking to me he said, "I just wish this wasn't going to be so difficult for you and the kids."

His request came in a quiet whisper and was delivered through a quivering bottom lip. "I just don't want to be forgotten."

It is my deepest honor to keep him in our living consciousness.

Forever.

* * *

The most meaningful space I hold is in my mind and heart. That is the true tribute I give to George.

I give him time almost every day—I talk to him and let him know what the plans are for the day, what each of the children are doing, and how very much we miss him.

And when, in conversation there is a memory, a saying, or some way George would fit into our conversations, we are now comfortable (myself, children, some family, and select friends) freely speaking his name… and that feels so very good.

It feels right.

What "Holding Space" Ultimately Means
By creating and holding space for George in my own unique ways, I have demonstrated to my children, friends, family, and myself that love never dies. Honoring those we have lost is both respectful and healthy.

I was also able to answer all my own questions about holding space. A person can create her own unique way of holding space. It does not have to be a set holiday or a prescribed format.

The more I leaned into and accepted the multitude of "spaces" I was holding for George, the more people who came into my home looked forward to seeing and hearing about these spaces.

As for how long you "hold space," that is a personal decision, and I am sure it will be dictated by each individual's rhythm of grief.

Chapter 12

Learning to Date After a Loss

Beginning to Date Again—and More Questions
In the early days of my "widowhood," my mind could only focus on my day-to-day activities, like making sure I was breathing. There wasn't any room in my thoughts to consider anything but how much I had lost and how much I was missing a part of myself.

It took me a long time before I felt like an individual. The thought of "moving on" from George was not a valid option. But I felt a transition in my being and began to think in terms of "moving forward."

As my grieving experience approached two and a half years, the thought of dating crept into my consciousness. That is the point at which I began to wonder if I could really date someone. It was an emotionally slow and painful process.

I didn't want to leave George behind, but I also felt a desire to share my life with someone. With a little more time, I began to believe that dating could be a real option.

I missed having a special person by my side. But who was I going to date? How was I going to find a date? How do I date? These were all very important questions.

I turned to online dating apps.

The learning curve was steep, intimidating, and at times, daunting. I found myself jumping from app to app, creating a profile, uploading, then editing the profile, and endlessly second-guessing every word.

But in the end, I did go on a few dates.

A Late Morning Coffee Date: My First Date
When my friends and family learned I was considering dating, they cautioned me about safety. I was also warned about giving out too much information and reminded of news stories about widows and widowers being scammed—or worse.

With all of that advice swimming in my brain, mixed with the memories of George and the guilt of even considering a date, I was terrified to go on this simple late-morning coffee outing.

I learned that with online dating, a first meeting is usually in a public place. That worked wonderfully with my next plan.

To combat my fears, I requested that my friend, her husband, and my two sisters-in-law to secretly accompany me. Perhaps this was unconventional, but it eased my nerves so that I could walk through the door to meet a stranger.

My posse of chaperones and I arrived early and we strategically placed ourselves around the coffeehouse.

My date arrived. The two of us ordered our coffee and sat at a table conveniently surrounded by my invisible safety net.

Many thoughts kept running through my mind: my chaperones were nearby, my date had no idea how many people were actually on this outing with him, and constant comparisons of him to George were pounding my brain. It was nearly impossible to focus on the actual conversation.

The gentleman was kind and courteous. I don't remember my date's name, and he never knew we had been chaperoned.

* * *

Journal Entry – October 2022 – Grief Trigger During a Date (Four years after his death)

A friendly dinner, a fire outside, and drinks. Getting to know one another seemed easy, conversation was flowing, and we were relaxing into the date.

As we refreshed our drinks, a small, considerate gesture pulled an unknown and unforeseen grief trigger—collapsing the atmosphere into something from which I needed to escape.

The trigger? A tender touch as he moved the clasp of my necklace from the front to the back of my neck. An innocent touch.

Raising my gaze to meet his eyes in gratitude, I expected to see caramel eyes, instead, I looked into warm blue eyes.

I was shocked. Momentarily, I froze. My brain re-engaged, my lips firmed, and my smile returned. I thanked this gentleman for his kind act, as my mind was planning my escape.

Escape from sharing information, escape from feeling connected, and escape from an event in which I no longer wanted to play a part. This man did nothing wrong. He was perfectly pleasant. The problem was my mind.

I expected to see George. Instead, I saw a stranger who had no knowledge of who I was or how I came to be the way I am.

* * *

Dating While Still Loving My Deceased Husband
Each date has a story.

Some of those stories are funny, sad, or disappointing, but what I find fascinating is the fact that I sometimes called my dates by my husband's name. While understandable, that is a little weird, even for me.

George is the name of my husband—he's dead, but still my husband. I am pretty sure the mistake of calling someone by the name of a familiar person has some psychological root based on familiarity and repetition.

After all, for twenty-three years of marriage (plus another year of knowing each other), when my husband brought me a cup of coffee or a cocktail, I would say, "Thank you, George." If you think about it, if George brought me a cup of coffee and a cocktail, and I said, "Thank you, George," each time, five days a week, for twenty-four years, that's a lot of repetition.

Doing the math, that's a minimum of 12,480 "Thank you, George" statements. That's if we only had one cocktail and one cup of coffee during each of the five nights a week. So, I can confidently say that my brain formed a strong habit of saying George's name over the twenty-four years I knew him.

A New Companion

There is a gentleman I am seeing regularly. His name is Ernie. My kids like Ernie. He's kind, funny, gentle, handsome, and wholeheartedly accepts George–his memory, and permanent place in our lives.

Even after two years of dating, when I start to say "Ernie" in my mind–before I open my mouth–I still think, "George." Next, I think, "No, this is Ernie," then I speak. I can see the humor and the rationalization of why I still have this mental process, but it can be uncomfortable and awkward at times.

It is a lightning-fast mental interchange, but still, it occurs.

Ernie is gracious and reassures me that he feels I am inadvertently complimenting him. He smiles and hugs me.

* * *

Folding Cranes and Healing Hearts
Dating was not the only way grief shifted in me. As my grieving evolves, the ways I hold space for those I loved and lost have changed over time.

As I have grown and moved through the healing process, I have learned to accept the flow and rhythm needed to grieve and to honor the loved ones I have lost.

I have learned to embrace the changes.

During the first months after George died, we–family and friends–were all deeply grieving.

Emma was thirteen and newly fatherless; she withdrew into her mind, into her bedroom, and away from me.

I was trying my best to keep the family a family. I spoke with Emma and explained that I thought we should try to spend a little time together.

She agreed.

We decided to take a community education class, origami on Saturday mornings. We had a little fun, and scheduling time together was good for our relationship. We rode our bikes to class and created some new memories.

Origami is the Japanese art of folding paper. The class began the fall after George's death. Our teacher's name was Cocoa. She instructed us on how to make a flower, a box, and a crane.

I was particularly drawn to the crane. It was beautiful. Even more beautiful was the Senbazuru that Cocoa shared with the class. Senbazuru is an ancient Japanese legend promising a wish to anyone folding 1,000 cranes.

My heart leapt at hearing this story. I immediately went to the craft store and purchased origami paper, deciding that I would fold 1,000 cranes by the first anniversary of George's death. I would make a wish for my heart to heal.

I folded cranes while drinking my coffee, getting ready for work, at lunch, in meetings, and watching television. With each fold of every crane, I thought of my Honey Bunny and how my heart needed to heal. It was meditative.

I made and continuously updated a chart of the cranes completed versus cranes still needing to be folded. The project gave me something positive on which to concentrate while I was intensely grieving.

I stored the completed cranes in a beautiful, ornate wooden chest–just large enough to hold all the cranes.

The 1,000 crane-folding project was completed on time, and I made my wish on April 15, 2019.

I experienced an unanticipated, but appreciated, sense of accomplishment. While my heart injury remained, a great amount of soothing and healing did take place.

On New Year's Eve the following year, I burned my 1,000 cranes in memory of my Honey Bunny, George Fredrick Braun, whom I will love always.

Chapter 13

Forgiveness

...and the First Waves of Guilt

Journal Entry – April 18, 2018 (Three days after his death)

I know I can't change anything I've said or done and just hope that you forgive me for my mistakes and hope you realized before you died, how I totally loved you. As I was getting older, I was getting better at loving you.

* * *

What is there to forgive? Or rather, what is there not to forgive? That is more how it felt almost immediately following the funeral.

After George's death, I would replay doctor visits, re-read medical consults, and second-guess every decision I made and helped George make while he was alive. Through his illness, I tried so hard to do everything I could to save his life.

The energy I had been using trying to save his life was diverted and focused with laser precision. What was I doing with my laser focused energy? I was reliving the last twenty months and finding all the mistakes that were made.

It was a spiraling descent into guilt. You would think I would have been able to take a breath and relax into the comfort of knowing that I tried my best, but that isn't what happened. This was not a conscious thought process.

* * *

Journal Entry – July 7, 2018 (Three months after his death)

You repeatedly stated that you were glad it was you who had cancer and were dying instead of me.

While you were alive, I could not bring myself to acknowledge that selfless act of pure love.

I didn't want it to be you, nor did I want it to be me.

Does it make me a bad person that I did not want to exchange places with you?

* * *

During a crisis or major event, my go-to knee-jerk reaction is to tell everyone what has happened and to "circle the wagons" of support. Often it may appear like a "party"–lots of people, food, and drink. Lots of conversation. Remember the coffin-assembly "event?"

The day George was diagnosed with cancer was no different. I immediately called my best friend, Odalis. She called the "Village" (a group of social friends), and they prepared a dinner gathering to show support.

Well, I failed to ask George if that was what he wanted. For the incredibly sensitive and empathetic person I am, I cannot, still to this day, believe how insensitive I was. It was his cancer; it was his life. George didn't want a "Village gathering," but he went along with it.

We talked that evening after the "Village" left. He explained his feelings, and I could not have felt worse. That was my first of many missteps through his treatment and transition to death.

* * *

Journal Entry – December 2018 (Eight months after his death)

I have bouts of regret. Was I loving enough? I should have sat with you more, just held your hand, just shared space. I was so focused on caregiving, I sometimes left out the 'loving.'

* * *

I thought our lives were busy when we were just "trucking along" before cancer. But when you add normal life activities to also getting ready to die… it is quite the lethal combination (pun intended).

Doctor appointments to arrange, cancel, and attend. Lab results to interpret and confirm. Rides to and from school for Emma. Grocery shopping, plane reservations, rental cars, food preparation, house cleaning, pet watching, and clothes washing. Oh, don't forget paying bills, keeping track of the cash flow, and properly notifying family and friends of the latest progress or lack thereof of George's treatment.

* * *

I Wasn't Ready

To let you go

To feel my soul torn as you died

To live my life without you

To feel my love grow for you even after your death

To see your body move into the flames

–EJ Braun

* * *

Feelings? Who had time for feelings or emotions? We just had things to do until after the funeral.

After the funeral, there was plenty of time–

Time to think.

Time to feel.

Time to remember.

In my mind, I began to run through the twenty months of diagnosis, treatments, travel, bad news, good news, and interactions. I remembered everything, every single thing I said or did wrong. Let me emphasize *wrong*. I remembered over and over again, replaying the moments in my brain.

Diagnosis day was bad, but so were the many days when our hopes were crushed. And then the actual death– my Honey Bunny's last breath. My guttural, and soul-wrenching moan as he exhaled for the last time.

To see and feel those moments once is heartbreaking. To replay those moments in my brain over and over with perfect clarity–that is torture.

* * *

Grief Cloud

Grief looks like drinkin' on Tuesdays
Grief looks like vacuuming the couch

Forgetting all your things
But remembering everything

Well I remember everything
I remember everything

Grief looks like
Crying at colors

Grief looks like
Not crying at all

So afraid to forget
But not scared to die

Stay busy to keep alive
That heap on the floor will not help you survive

Only so many push-ups a girl can do
Each one takes me further away
From you

–Lexi Braun

* * *

One vivid memory that haunts me was a time when George began to vomit about five minutes after he had taken all of his morning medications. Sitting on the edge of the bed, he was about to vomit on the bed sheets, and I said, "Honey, grab the trash can." (The trash can was right next to him; all he had to do was move his hand about two inches.)

I really didn't think he could hear me over the noise of his retching stomach. So I raised my voice. He retched again, and I raised my voice even more.

Through his retching and my raising my voice, he was able to grab the trash can and move it closer to his mouth. Between vomiting and wiping his mouth, and in a tone that reminded me of a little boy, he asked, "Why are you yelling at me?"

I still wince when I think of how the tone of my voice made him feel.

Here was this wonderful man, neck dissected, suffering through chemotherapy and radiation, getting thinner by the day, pretty much dying before my eyes, though trying to survive–and I was raising my voice about five tablespoons of vomit.

In a twenty-month period, there are many stories and scenarios in which I did not do or say the right things, was irritated, or responded in a way that I would never consider "okay." Cancer, illness, and giving full-time care to the sick–they have a life of their own.

What happened and how it happened, I will never forget. I am not here to fall on the sword and confess to all the incidents in which I should have reacted better or behaved differently, but I am here to say, "I am human."

Whether helping a loved one die or experiencing their sudden death, a person may feel deep regret over their own imperfections, or the imperfections in their relationship.

Humans make mistakes.

* * *

Journal Entry – November 2017 (Six months before his death)

I worry about my intense focus on George, how that limits my time with Emma, and what effect this will have on her mental and emotional stability.

Chapter 14

Trauma and Mental Warfare

The constant replay of this "movie of regret" is not un-common. It is a response to trauma. I recognized it from my career as a firefighter/paramedic, and it is the familiar psychological response that I continue to have to some of the most impactful 9-1-1 calls I worked on.

There is one particular call, a motor vehicle accident, that I continue to work through in my mind and emotions. I have learned to embrace this call, and I would like to take you through the memory.

My fire department services a mid-sized city. I was the fire lieutenant at a small station on the outskirts of town. A driver-operator and a firefighter were on duty with me. We were asleep in the early morning hours and awakened by the alarm tones.

The Accident

Our unit was dispatched to a vehicle accident involving extrication. This meant that more units would be assigned to help cut apart the car and free any entrapped victims.

The accident was in my immediate territory—a short distance from the station. We all jumped in the engine. My driver verified the address, and I began verbalizing our duties en route to the call.

My unit arrived, and I made my arrival report over the radio to inform the other responding units that there were three patients in one car, two of whom appeared to be "Signal 7" (deceased). All occupants of the second car appeared uninjured and were out of their vehicle.

The extrication unit arrived. I pointed them to the most likely survivor, the driver, for extrication. I went to reassess the other two passengers (young teenage girls) in the same vehicle (one was in the front passenger seat and the other in the rear passenger seat). That's when I saw what appeared to be *another* person cradling the patient in the back seat. There were now *four* patients. I updated all arriving units that there was an additional patient.

The District Chief arrived on the scene. We walked to the car together and counted the patients together. We looked in the back seat. There was clearly only one patient in the back seat. I apologized for the mistake, and we continued to work the scene to save the only living person in this car, the driver.

Amongst the smell of blood, alcohol, brain matter, and smoke, I thought, "How could I make that mistake?"

There are moments in life that will replay in your mind forever. For me, this motor vehicle accident is one of those life moments.

* * *

When my mind replays this incident, I also see the fearful looks on the faces of the uninjured occupants of the second vehicle, knowing that they are emotionally scarred for life. It does not matter that it wasn't their fault. The driver and the kids who were in that car experienced the accident and saw what they saw.

* * *

Journal Entry – September 2018 (Five months after his death)

Deep breath… one moment. Please. I have to remember I could never have controlled or predicted this outcome. Calm my soul and comfort myself, because deep down, I am a good person with a good soul and mean no harm.

* * *

You may be thinking: "What was Betty's mistake?" or "For what does she need to forgive herself?" or perhaps, "Why in hell is she telling this story?"

This story is a demonstration of the psychological replay, the unconsciously self-imposed mental warfare that a person may go through when trauma is experienced. I did nothing wrong. I made no mistakes (I will return to the miscounting of patients in the next chapter), and yet this replaying loop continues, years after the event.

In the days, weeks, and months immediately following the accident, the entire call would replay in my mind without warning at lightning speed. I could not control when, or how many times in rapid succession the replay would occur.

Over ten years later, I can still conjure this event and bring it to the forefront of my consciousness. With it come the smells and images, as clear as when I was experiencing the call. At this juncture in my life, I can also release the emotion and talk about the call without "re-experiencing" the event.

Learning to create emotional distance from the memory takes time.

This is the point I am making. You may be reliving the entire event of a loved one's diagnosis through death—this is normal. These "replays" may cause intense regret of your actions or non-actions during the course of the loss of your loved one. The guilt can be overwhelming.

You cannot take away what you have done, seen, or said, nor can you change the outcome. However, a person can learn to understand what is occurring.

If a person stays stuck in the replaying of her imperfections, grief may only intensify. My answer to that is forgiveness. Forgiveness of self, of others, and for perceived mistakes. This can help the mind to move toward a place of peace, to fully embrace our humanity and to preserve sanity.

Reaching out to a trauma or grief counselor can help.

* * *

"Grief never ends, but it changes.

It is a passage, not a place to stay.

Grief is not a sign of weakness nor a lack of faith;

It is the price of love."

–Author Unknown

* * *

Journal Entry – May 12, 2018 (Three weeks after his death)

I have figured out that it was a dying wish of yours to get a Jeep. I'm so sorry, I am so very dense. Please forgive me.

* * *

Journal Entry – May 20, 2018 (Four weeks after his death)

I know I can't stay in the same space forever. I am taking baby steps… They are hard steps.

* * *

Journal Entry – March 2021 (Three years after his death)

My family is my center–yet I feel detached, uninterested, and disengaged from almost every event. Where I once would be the organizer and last to leave events, now I show up out of obligation and leave as soon as possible.

Will I ever want to reconnect?

As my family is experiencing their individual trials, I find my own heart closed. I don't feel the energy to get involved. Hypocritical is how I feel.

I accepted their love and assistance when George was sick, after he died, and while I was re-establishing my life.

I can't seem to make space in my heart.

I know they know I love them.

Am I turning to stone? I want to be needed, to help, to fix … What is wrong with me?

Maybe, just maybe, nothing is wrong with me.

Maybe this is my best right now. My best feels so different in this phase of my life.

* * *

I needed a framework for forgiveness that I could understand, that wasn't placating my emotional state. It came from an unexpected place.

Years ago, when I was still a teacher, I sought counseling to help me mentally deal with a specific case of a student's child abuse. My counselor understood me well and suggested that I might find some comfort in the message of the movie *Smoke Signals*.

Timing is everything. I came across this movie again, after George died.

* * *

Smoke Signals is about forgiveness. The movie is based on a book by Sherman Alexie. It is about an angry, coming-of-age young man.

The boy's father was an alcoholic who physically and verbally abused his family. He also caused their financial ruin and then abandoned the family. The boy grew up angry at his father and at life, and when he became a young man, he was sent to retrieve his dead father's ashes.

The young man had every right to be angry. But his unresolved anger only brought more discontent to his life, the life of his mother, and his friends.

At the powerful hinge point in the movie, when the young man is raging out of control, the narrator askes, "What is left, if we forgive our fathers?"

Love. Love is the only thing left after forgiveness.

* * *

Forgiveness and love are healing forces that allow a person to move freely with grief as it morphs and changes.

Chapter 15

What Happens When You Die?

This chapter is not about answers; it is about how I learned to live with questions.

There is an abundance of theories trying to account for death and what happens to the energy that has vacated the body. After all, energy is neither created nor destroyed, so where does it go?

Do I have the answer? I do have *an* answer. This is an answer I have created for myself, based on my life experiences, books I have read, lessons I have learned from sermons, and stories I have listened to.

To tell you the truth, my "answer" has changed as I have gotten older; I can only imagine it will continue to change until the day I die.

* * *

"There's More Than One Way To Skin A Cat."
That was one of Mom's frequent sayings, my favorite.

Do you remember as a young child just knowing there is a right and wrong?

I do.

In fact, I remember naively thinking that our neighbor, in Jackson, New Jersey, made iced tea the wrong way.

Luckily, I confided to my mother, at the tender age of about seven, that Vern Vern's mother (Yes, we called him "Vern Vern" and he was my childhood playmate until we moved from New Jersey) made iced tea incorrectly.

My gentle-souled mother lowered her shoulders and softened her stance at the kitchen sink, turned to me, and quietly explained that there are many ways to make iced tea.

"Betty Jean," she said softly, "a person isn't wrong because she has a different way of doing things." Mom continued, "You may find that as you grow up and try new foods or activities that you may like different things–that you do not like right now."

I turned and ran out the door, happy that Vern Vern's mom wasn't wrong. I had no idea I had just been taught about tolerance and acceptance, and that I would use and refer to that lesson throughout my entire life.

Mom's Take on Religion

I became a "saved," "born-again Christian" when I was in eighth grade. I was "saved" during a non-denominational church event held in a converted garage in Stuart, Florida. I remember feeling proud about being saved.

Mom said, "That's great, Betty Jean… let me ask you a question. Do you really think that there is only one religion that is 'right'?"

While she did not utter my favorite phrase at that specific moment, Mom continued. "You have to use your head, Betty Jean. Would God send people, innocent people, who never heard of Christianity, to Hell, just because they didn't know about God? What about good-hearted people who grew up without religion? Why would they go to Hell?"

Mom let me be "saved" as long as I wanted to be saved.

She allowed me to include prayers before each dinner, not just our customary prayers before a holiday meal. She prevented my sister Fran (four years older than me) from beating me up when I would say "Hallelujah," because I was grateful for something.

But she put her foot down in a very stern way when I was writing to a friend whose older brother tragically died in a motorcycle accident.

As I was writing out my sympathy card, she said, "Betty Jean, do not write in your card anything like, 'This was God's plan.' Don't you dare."

I was shocked. She knew *exactly* what I intended to write, and it made me sad to think that I was going to do something that Mom thought was inappropriate.

It wasn't until I was an adult, teaching high school science, and experienced the death of two of my former students that I understood what would have been the mistake of my intended words of sympathy. Mom–so wise, so gentle, so beautiful. I miss Mom.

Childhood Nighttime Talks at the Dining Room Table
At night, when the adults and older siblings were gathered around the dinner table–and I was supposed to be in bed–I would sit on the upstairs landing, secretly listening to what the adults had to say.

The conversations were very informative. I learned their opinions on religion, politics, death, angels, life after death, Santa Claus, and the Easter Bunny too.

As I grew older, I had my own space at the nighttime table talk. I remember someone saying she had a dream about a person–and then later received a phone call that the same person in her dream was either sick or injured. Another relative woke in the middle of the night to see a deceased family member sitting at the foot of the bed.

These stories came from my family, whom I trust and believe implicitly.

I spent a lot of time on my own–outside, playing, thinking, and dreaming. I was comfortable being by myself or with friends. Mom, one time in my upbringing, pointed out that I had great confidence and that I seemed okay if people didn't agree with me.

This remains true, most of the time. What I am saying is that these are *my* thoughts in this book—and it's perfectly acceptable if you don't resonate with everything I write. My rhythm is mine alone. This sets the stage for the next few real-life stories.

A Visit from Mom

As an adult, I personally witnessed a birthday balloon move on its own after my daughter's thirteenth birthday party. Reading that sentence makes my nose crinkle with suspect curiosity.

Mom had recently died in December, 2017. My daughter's birthday was just over a month later.

The party had concluded, and it was only me, my daughter, and George sitting in the living room, watching a movie on the television. I saw something move out of the corner of my eye. I turned my head to look. I saw the balloon floating around the entire perimeter of the living room ceiling.

The fan was not on, nor was the air conditioner or heater.

The three of us watched the balloon.

As it made its way behind us—still at the ceiling level—it slowly descended to rest on the floor behind the couch where our daughter was sitting.

Angels, spirits, imagination? Our best guess was that it was Mom, wishing her granddaughter a happy birthday.

An Angel
The one time I believe I actually saw an angel was on one of the worst calls I worked as a fire lieutenant/paramedic.

If you remember, I recounted the gruesome motor vehicle accident in which two passengers were killed (they were young teenagers) and the adult driver almost died. I had initially reported that there were three patients in one car. When dispatch requested confirmation on the number of patients, I walked over to the car and counted again. I saw someone I did not initially see in the back seat–spooning /cradling the young patient whom I originally saw. In the end, however, there were only three patients.

* * *

These horrific tragedies have lasting effects on first responders. We are encouraged to participate in a form of group counseling called Critical Incident Stress Debriefing (CISD) to help manage the memories.

* * *

About a week or two after the call, we reported for a CISD session. First responders who were on the call that night were there, along with a chaplain, members of the communications division (dispatch), and additional first responders who had previous experience with this kind of mental trauma.

The emotions that filled the room were thick and raw. We were each asked what we saw and what our function was on this call. We did not have to speak. There was a lot of anger toward the adult driver, who caused the accident. It was difficult for some of the most experienced responders to talk without their voices cracking.

I had not intended to address the "fourth patient," but the fourth patient was brought up by a seasoned flight nurse who had not been on the call. She was one of the "additional" first responders and had read the transcript of the radio traffic as well as the incident reports.

This seasoned flight nurse looked at me and asked me what I saw. It took some time for me to let the words move through my lips... we're supposed to be strong, tough firefighters... but once I started my story, the words fell out of my mouth, along with tears.

This room was filled with an amount of testosterone that I would imagine in a coming-of-age elephant—and that elephant was here, figuratively speaking.

They were all listening to my story of how I saw something that was, by all accounts, unseeable.

The flight nurse who asked me to speak waited patiently until I finished my account of the call. She waited until people around the room wiped their eyes, then asked me, "Do you know what it was that you saw?" With reassurance, she was smiling. There I was, afraid of my perceived mistake of counting the number of patients, afraid to show emotion... because we all know, to spoof an old line from the movie *A League of Their Own*, "There's no crying in firefighting." And she was smiling through her own tears.

My mental answer to her question was, "Yes, I think I saw an angel!"

My voiced answer to her question was, "No."

Still smiling and looking directly into my eyes, ensuring I didn't miss her words, she said, "You saw an angel." My eyes filled up and then spilled over.

She looked around the room and said, "We see them all the time." She continued, "We see them comforting and guiding people as they die." Her smile grew larger.

I believe I had witnessed an angel.

Questions I Cannot Answer
Why don't we see angels all the time? Why did I not see George's angel, or my mother's angel? Why do some people see angels and others don't?

What you believe is what you believe. I am only stating what I saw and what I believe it was that I saw.

Do you believe in heaven, hell, or reincarnation? Are you agnostic or atheist? It doesn't matter to me. "You do you." "I'll do me."

But we all will grieve.

Chapter 16

What's So Funny?

This chapter epitomizes one of my survival techniques: one laugh at a time.

What is so funny about death? Well, nothing... but I can—and will—find humor in most every situation. I'm pretty sure, if you've read the previous chapters, you can tell that my heart and soul were broken with my loss of George.

I am not trying to minimize his death or the extent to which his death has impacted the lives of his family and friends. There were some humorous and funny moments during his twenty-month battle trying to fend off cancer.

These moments unfolded at different times during George's transition to death. The first took place in Lake Tahoe, just after he completed his chemotherapy and radiation treatments, the second occurred about two weeks before his death, and the final story came from the night he died.

Tahoe Ho Ho and the Angry Snowplow Driver
The 2016 Christmas-to-New Year's trip in Lake Tahoe continues to bring our family together through laughter. There are many stories to tell from this trip.

Which story should I tell?

The "Holiday Sleigh Ride" that involved no snow and a sleigh on wheels that took us through a parking lot? Or maybe how my daughter took "one last ski run" on the second day of skiing and broke both of her wrists? Perhaps I should tell you about the two earthquakes we experienced in the middle of the night.

I am going to focus on the end of our trip. The day we *left* Lake Tahoe… during a developing blizzard.

Seventeen of our family members were involved in this "once-in-a-lifetime family trip." In essence, we were a traveling group of fifteen able-bodied people and two that needed physical assistance.

George had completed his chemotherapy and radiation treatments only six weeks before our Christmas Day flight out west. Understandably, he was not in his normal mental or physical shape. While Mom, at age 82, still had her mental acuity and sense of humor, her body was failing. She required assistance.

Our family of seventeen did not have identical travel itineraries. Some traveled through Reno, Nevada, while others traveled through San Francisco, California. I was in the San Francisco group of nine people and two rental cars.

While we were packing up and preparing to leave the ski condominium it began to lightly snow. It was beautiful, even as the flurries came down thicker and faster.

The group I was in traveled south through town to traverse the pass to get to San Francisco. As the blizzard continued to develop, traffic began moving slower and visibility became limited.

We forged ahead only to find the pass out of Lake Tahoe closed due to heavy snow accumulation. All cars and trucks were turned around by law enforcement. We made the decision to back track through Lake Tahoe, stop to rest in Reno, then continue to San Francisco. While it wasn't the quickest route, it was the only route to our airport of departure. It was slow driving.

We had a very late dinner in Reno and rested for a few hours in a hotel. Around 2 a.m., our group decided to make our way to San Francisco. Getting on the highway, we were stopped at a safety checkpoint. The check point was to ensure vehicles getting on the highway could safely handle the snow accumulation. We considered putting snow chains on the sedan, but the checkpoint guy said the car and SUV we were traveling in should not have a problem. The car had front-wheel drive and the SUV had four-wheel drive.

The snowbanks on either side of the road were at least as tall as the vehicles. The sight was incredible. It was difficult to distinguish between the lanes on the highway. The lane lines were covered with thick layers of snow. We were very happy when we came up behind a snowplow and hoped it would drive straight to San Francisco.

We never knew how far the snowplow traveled because the windshield wiper fluid in the sedan ran out, the defroster malfunctioned, and the wipers froze onto the windshield, rendering visibility to zero.

The only way Cindy, the driver of the sedan, could see where she was going was to open the window and stick her head out of the car. We were forced to leave the highway at the first off-ramp that would lead us to an open gas station.

Exiting the highway, the snowbanks got much taller than the car, and the road became narrow from the buildup of snow that previous snowplows had scraped off the road. It was dark, cold, icy, and eerily quiet.

We drove down the off-ramp and saw the name of the road we were traveling to: Donner's Pass Road. I am not a history expert, but I do know the story of Donner's Pass; it didn't end well for the Donner family.

We spotted the fueling station and made a beeline for it— sort of.

As we headed down the off-ramp and stopped at the intersection, we saw that the fueling station was directly across the street, but up a hill. As our first vehicle, the one without windshield wipers, tried to make it up the hill, the car began to spin its wheels.

I exited the SUV to push the car and help it gain traction. My efforts worked. Added bonus: I ended up face down on the snow-covered road.

In retrospect, we should have applied the snow chains at the "Check Point."

To recap: we arrived in Lake Tahoe with two people needing physical assistance (George and Mom) and left with three. I wasn't kidding, Emma Jean had broken both of her wrists. Imagine an 11-year-old pre-teen athlete who could not use her hands for even the most basic tasks.

It continued to snow. We pulled into the gas station and took shelter under an overhang that provided some protection to one of the gas pump islands. As we were solving the problem of how to make the windshield wipers work (all we needed was to add more wiper fluid), George walked up to the front of the sedan and calmly stated, "The SUV has a flat."

Truly–the SUV had a flat tire. Perfect.

We were going to be there a little longer than anticipated.

I ushered my mom, Emma, and Owen (Emma's cousin) into the gas station for warmth. The rest of us remained outside, attempting to fix the car problems. Petra, a member of our group, was holding the snow chains for the sedan and talking with Cindy. George, JoAnne and Gabriele were trying to release the spare tire from the frozen undercarriage of the SUV.

A snowplow–not the same one we had been following–headed into the parking area.

I returned to the cars in time to hear the snowplow driver start yelling in our direction.

To understand the scenario: there were no other cars in the parking lot, no other patrons; ours were the only two vehicles in the area until the snowplow arrived.

The driver appeared extremely angry and flailed his arms at us to move the vehicles.

Cindy, our spokesperson who is very calm in tense situations, approached the angry snowplow driver. She attempted to explain the problems we were having but the man abruptly interrupted her by yelling that we had to move. When we moved the vehicles to the next island the snowplow driver became incensed.

His reaction was confusing. Each of us scanned the parking lot to see if we were missing something. Cindy decided she needed to have another talk with the driver and began to walk in his direction.

As she was trying to calm the snowplow driver, I called over to Cindy from the building and asked the location of Petra. Petra had become our fourth casualty needing assistance. She had developed a high fever and needed to lie down in the back of the SUV. (Petra later ended up with a diagnosis of mononucleosis).

Cindy was still trying to figure out what the snowplow driver needed to stop his foul ranting. He was nowhere near calm, and apparently, did not appreciate Cindy's ability to remain calm under pressure.

As the snowplow driver was yelling through his open window, snow was flying in his face, and his face had turned red. Cindy gave up on talking to this person and began to walk away. He screamed at her, saying he was going to call the police. This threat made Cindy turn on her heel and yell right back at him, "Go ahead, I WANT you to call the police, we need help!"

What pushed the driver over his emotional edge was Cindy's loudly voiced rhetorical question: "Why do you have to be such an ASSHOLE?!"

The snowplow driver flung open the cab door. I immediately left my post and moved to my sister's side, grabbing the tire iron as I walked past the SUV.

I figured that if he was going to attack Cindy, he was going to have to attack both of us.

The driver jumped down from his cab onto the parking lot.

As his feet landed on the snow-packed asphalt, all conversation came to an immediate halt.

Cindy and I looked *down* at him. We then looked at each other.

Now that the driver was on the ground, he had to look *up* at us.

The snowplow driver was not more than four feet, five inches tall. Cindy is five feet eleven inches tall, and I am five feet eight inches tall. I think he saw the smirk on our faces, as we began to understand the reality that his stature did not match the size of his bark.

He suddenly climbed back into his cab and drove away.

Our smirks turned to laughter.

That moment of laughter seemed to break our streak of everything going wrong. About three minutes after the snowplow driver tucked his tail and drove off, a tow-truck entered the fueling station. Dawn was breaking and it stopped snowing.

The driver of the tow-truck approached us and offered to access the spare tire. He knew how to circumvent the iced mechanism. In addition, he changed the tire for us.

His name was Michael. We will never forget our guardian angel who swooped in to help us. Yes, his name really was Michael.

* * *

Before Cancer

When George was home, healthy and alive, our morning routine began with giggles as we woke up and shared the dreams we had the night before.

We would share the morning duties. One of us would make coffee while the other let out the dogs, fed the cats, and opened the chicken coop.

George would pour the coffee and doctor it up with generous amounts of sugar and cream until it was just right. We would walk out onto our back porch, sit on the swing, and watch the chickens peck the ground, swinging slowly as we sipped our caffeine until it was time to wake up our youngest for school.

What a wonderful montage of memories.

As George's Cancer Progressed

We consciously maintained our normal family routines for as long as possible. These included, but were not limited to, our morning coffee ritual and driving Emma Jean to school as a family.

I was so fortunate that my fire department shift work was covered by my co-workers, allowing me to stay home and care for George during the last several weeks of his life.

As he ate less, moved less, and talked less, we made a concerted effort to laugh more.

Are You Sure You Want Coffee? (About two weeks before his death)

We had moved our caffeine-sipping coffee moments inside the house because it took too much energy for George to ambulate outside. I was doing the morning chores and making the coffee as my Honey Bunny expended his precious energy to get up and walk to the living room.

By the time I had completed the morning chores and prepared the coffee, he was sitting on the couch, perched and ready.

We went through this routine every day for quite a few days before I noticed he had not been drinking his coffee—not a drop.

The very next morning, as the routine was getting started, I asked him, "Honey, are you sure you want coffee this morning?" His response: "Yes, please!" Me: "Okay!"

As we chatted, I kept an eye on his coffee level. Still, he was not drinking any.

When we were done, I would gather the mugs and other items, take them to the kitchen, and pour all that cream, sugar and coffee from George's mug down the drain.

In truth, I am not sure how many days this went on, but it was enough for me to notice.

One morning, as I was placing the mugs in the sink, I didn't empty George's completely full coffee mug. Instead, I placed it in the refrigerator.

The next morning, I made the morning coffee and completed the morning chores.

George mustered the energy to dress and sit in the living room.

I fixed my cup of fresh coffee, and as I walked to the living room, I grabbed his coffee from the refrigerator and lovingly placed it on the side table next to my Honey Bunny.

Guess what? He didn't touch the mug; he had no idea I served him a mug of cold coffee from the day before.

This went on for three days.

After day three of my "experiment," I asked George if he wanted me to continue making him a mug of coffee in the morning. "Yesssiree," was his reply.

I responded with laughter. He started snickering–not knowing why, but because we enjoyed laughing together.

He asked, "What's so funny?"

I could hardly speak through my belly laugh.

I finally stopped laughing enough to say, "Do you realize your coffee is ice cold? I've been repurposing your coffee every day and you haven't touched it."

We laughed and laughed together. He touched the side of the coffee mug to test my claim. He started laughing all over again.

By this time in his treatment, George was on so much fentanyl for pain that he would lose track of time. He said, "I really thought I was drinking it," and he chuckled some more.

The next morning, I served my Honey Bunny cold coffee, and we laughed until we cried.

* * *

No one should wait for tomorrow.

* * *

A Special and Profound Request– Paint My Toenails
We discussed his final wishes during our morning coffee–
or non-coffee–moments. During these conversations I was intent on taking notes so that I didn't forget anything.

George reiterated that he didn't want to be forgotten and he wanted to be cremated in his favorite Hawaiian shirt and tan shorts. I was the only one George wanted to be in the room when he died.

As he was slowly speaking, suddenly a little smile came into his eyes.

George paused and then told me that after he died, he wanted the children in the family to paint his toenails and for the adults to make a champagne toast.

I stopped writing, looked up at him, and saw his grin. I asked him, "What color polish would you like for the children to use?"

Again, he smiled and said, "Whatever feels right."

At first, I thought the request was "a little different." But I am the self-proclaimed queen of "odd." So, if Honey Bunny wanted his nails painted, he was going to get his nails painted.

I dutifully recorded his requests. Not until much later did I realize the everlasting positive effects it would have on the children as well as the adults.

Let's move on to the point in time after I was able to compose myself the evening George died.

We prepared Honey Bunny so that we could bring the children into the bedroom to see him. His body was washed and he was dressed in his requested shirt and shorts. I combed his hair.

Now, for the toenails. At first, the younger children were timid. Lexi recognized their hesitation and broke the ice by painting the first toenail. That's all it took for the children to jump in and help.

Emma chose a color but opted not to paint. I don't blame her.

The kids painted all the toenails. Some of the adults wanted to paint a nail as well, so we moved on to the fingernails.

We opened the champagne and toasted George—his life and the indelible mark his presence made on this earth.

Standing around my Honey Bunny, we shared stories, and champagne toasts. Taking in the whole scene, I was in awe of how handsome and peaceful George looked in death.

His requests were fulfilled, making the act of dying less frightening for the kids… and for the adults.

* * *

Excerpt from Cindy's memorial words at George's Celebration of Life:

"When he knew he would not survive this illness, he accepted it. George's worry was that his family would be okay.

He told Betty Jean that when he died, he wanted the kids to paint his toenails all different colors.

It seemed like kind of a weird request, but when the time came, we did it, and it made a heartbreaking and sad situation bearable–and actually fun and memorable for something other than the terrible loss and sadness we felt.

I can see his face smiling now, remembering when he told us that he wanted this done, all the while knowing the positive impact it was going to have on all of us."

* * *

Journal Entry – April 14, 2018 (The day before his death)

I wiped down his face with a warm damp washcloth, and we held hands for a few minutes.

I told him how much I appreciated how he looked after us, how much I loved him, and that we were going to be okay.

Although his face moved very little, I could tell he was smiling.

He was resting comfortably.

Lexi came in to say hello and good morning. She noticed his lips were dry, applied lip balm to his lips, and was silently crying while holding his hand.

Miraculously, he spoke, and asked her, "So, what's on my agenda today?" Lexi kiddingly replied, "A trip to Lowe's, an appointment at noon, and then go to the beach."

He replied, "It all sounds good except for the beach." Lexi told him she was teasing him.

He smiled, and we laughed through our tears.

* * *

The HELLO Nametag…The Night George Died

After the nail-polish activity, it was time to call the funeral home.

George passed away at 8:00 p.m. By the time I called the funeral home, it was about 10:00 p.m. I pulled out the paperwork to locate the phone number.

As I reread the final arrangement checklist, created by the funeral home and signed by me, I noticed that the box next to "embalming" was checked.

My eyes bugged out–George DID NOT want to be embalmed; he felt very strongly about it.

I made a call to the funeral home. The person who answered my call–calm, comforting, and appropriately somber–assured me that George would not be embalmed. Not willing to risk this final request slipping through the cracks, I asked to speak with Margaret, the person who helped me make all the original arrangements. The gentleman I spoke to acknowledged my request and said someone would call back.

The phone call ended and I frantically explained the paperwork snafu to my family. They, too, were trying to calm me.

I considered accompanying George to the funeral home to ensure no embalming mistake would occur.

A few minutes later, the phone rang. It was one of the two brothers who owned the business. He did not make me repeat my concern.

He immediately apologized for the paperwork mistake and explained that no embalming would take place that night, that it was not necessary for me to accompany my husband to the funeral home, and gave me his personal guarantee.

The owner asked that I call back when the family was ready for George to be picked up. I thanked him, and we ended the conversation.

At this point, I was fairly certain the funeral home would not embalm George, but I was still a little worried.

My friend Odalis and I went into the kitchen. Absent-mindedly, I rummaged through my kitchen junk drawer. I had intended to write a note instructing the funeral home staff not to embalm George, when I came across a clear plastic box of name tags. You know—the kind that says 'Hello, my name is…

These name tags had a white background and red print. I remember them well.

I picked up the box as I was explaining the situation and the note I intended to write.

Odalis was listening intently when I stopped in the middle of my sentence, looked at the box of name tags, and I softly chuckled. Not knowing exactly what I was thinking, Odalis began laughing with me.

The story ends with me placing a name tag on the left front pocket of George's shirt, that read, 'HELLO, my name is George.' Written underneath were the words: "Please do not embalm me."

I kissed my husband and explained the situation to the very kind men who came to retrieve George.

They smiled at the name tag, and the look in their eyes—filled with compassion—let me know they understood.

As promised, George was not embalmed.

Chapter 17

Finding Peace

There is not, and never will be, a guide or words of comfort that can reach the initial innermost fear, devastation, loneliness, and the overwhelming sense of annihilation that comes with death.

This book, obviously, is not an outline for navigating grief. There is no such entity. George and I were married for twenty-three years… we were still in love.

My comfort comes from the memories, the love I had and will always have, the knowledge that life has been wonderful, and the core belief that there is still more to do on this earth… those are the thoughts and feelings that can give a person the strength to lift one foot, then the other, to walk toward a new future… along with counting to ten.

* * *

Excerpt from Lexi's memorial words at George's Celebration of Life:

"On his last day, the day before he died, he caught me holding his hand and crying. He woke up out of nowhere and said, "What's with this woe-is-me stuff? Get on with what you've got to do!" And that's exactly what we're going to do: we'll keep teaching each other, keep on loving each other, and keep celebrating."

* * *

Layered Grief

Elizabeth Lucia Riggio Diven, my mother, was a beautiful person who had nothing but compassion and understanding for people. The love for her children, her pride in our accomplishments, childlike excitement for life, and the look of pure love in her eyes are all attributes I will remember. My mother died four months before George. There was no pause between those losses. When George became sick, I became his caregiver, and my grief for my mother was set aside. There was no time, no space, no energy left to tend to it. I didn't grieve her then. I compartmentalized. That grief waited. It surfaced later, layered into every life event that followed.

One. Step. At. A. Time.

My New Future

Grief was my world, and its right-hand partner was death. As you may well know, grieving is an all-encompassing, full-time job. Before I could envision and begin developing my "new" future, I first had to re-enter the living world.

Friends and family were kind and patient; no one pushed me to "move on." They were, however, mindful of my well-being. Consistently, I was invited to events–bike rides, birthday parties, hanging out at a lake house… distractions. Distractions from grief can be a slippery slope, especially if they are used to avoid feeling.

I noticed that my mind was beginning to crave a bifurcated trail. One side longed for the familiar comforts of a well-traveled path that required no thought to traverse. The other side of this "trail"–my new horizon, forced upon me by this involuntary change–offered little familiarity.

I have always liked and embraced change, yet this change felt like being spun blindfolded and dropped somewhere unknown.

My life is entirely new, yet glimpses of familiarity remain in my memories.

* * *

Silent Tears of Beauty

I found the silence I'm seeking

It is beautiful–nothing but the sounds of the earth

Waves

Winds

My heartbeat

And birds… the lovely song of passing birds

Here is where my tears can escape

Be accepted, absorbed, and transformed

The beauty of the dancing light on the melody of waves

I am alone, yet home and comforted

By the earth

–EJ Braun

* * *

Planting Seeds for Thought

In the early fall of 2019, my sister-in-law Donna was at my house visiting. This was the house that George and I had purchased from his mother.

We had gutted the house, moved walls, replaced the flooring, added a screened-in porch, and built what we considered the best chicken coop in the world. We knew the location of every pipe, nail, screw, and support beam in the house. We created our home.

During Donna's visit, I relived some of the remodel memories with her and shared that staying in the house was both difficult and comforting– a reflection of my bifurcated trail. Donna suggested that it might be time for me to move to a different house. I shrugged off the suggestion, as the thought of leaving that house made me sad.

But here's the neat part: the seed had been planted.

* * *

Journal Entry – January 2020 (Two years after his death)

Last week, I began preparing to move and change houses.

How did I decide it was time? The decision was multilayered, a natural progression, and at times very difficult. Although, when I was ready, the actual act of deciding was an easy, logical, and freeing experience.

A particular difficulty I had not anticipated occurred as my family and I dismantled George's well-thought-out and organized garage and tool bench. I felt as if I were dismantling a part of him… as if I was making him leave and sending him away.

I dealt with these feelings after everyone else left. I was alone to handle the final portion of this "dismantling."

I unrolled the poster of George and me that had been displayed at George's funeral (the funeral home had created it from one of the pictures we had submitted for a slide show during the celebration of life).

Many people signed the poster, and several left encouraging messages. I sat on the garage floor, opened the poster, and read each signature and every message. I cried and sobbed, allowing myself six minutes of full-on grieving for the loss of my husband and life I had known.

As I wiped away my tears and blew my nose, I carefully rolled up the poster and continued to pack. This house is no longer my life, but it will always represent my life with George. It was a good life.

* * *

Early December 2019 – How I Found My New Home
To get me out of seclusion and meet new people, Odalis had a friend invite me to a Christmas party. Odalis drove across town to pick me up and take me to the party. As we got closer to the address, I realized the house was in the same neighborhood as my sister Cindy and one of my nephews.

We pulled into the driveway and walked up the sidewalk to the front door. As the front door opened, I said to

Odalis, "I could live here." Crossing the threshold, I felt warmth, calmness, and peace. It felt like I was stepping into a comforting hug.

The owner, Leslie, replied, "We're planning to put the house on the market in January."

Sometimes, you just know.

The sale of my old house and the purchase of my new home were completed on the same day in April 2020, just before COVID shut down the world. I had never solely owned a parcel of land or a house. To add a cherry on top of this cake, George would have loved this house.

That seed Donna planted grew into one of the best decisions of my life, right behind marrying George, changing my career from teaching to firefighting, and adopting our daughter (listed in chronological order).

There will always be a tug in my heart when I remember the house George and I shared.

* * *

Journal Entry – September 2020 – Returning to My Past (Two years after his death)

As I lie sleepless in my bed, tears stream down my face. My tears are for a life I no longer live, a residual sadness that blisters my heart as my soul is healing.

At first, I was restless; then my stomach began to churn... It took a few minutes for me to feel the tears streaming down and staining my cheeks. My past had forced its way in, demanding my undivided attention.

My mind was frantic, trying to piece together the cause of my tears. Was it that I missed George? Was it that I had started dating? All of my immediate checks for life threats were negative. Then my old house flashed into consciousness.

Lightning struck my soul, and I began to weep. A deep, heaving, yet silent weeping overtook me, and I knew I had hit the mark. That afternoon, I had returned to our old street and had driven into our old neighborhood to look at the house we had made into our home.

* * *

Journal Entry – August 2020 – First vacation as a widow (Two years after his death)

I remember my first hike in Colorado with the "Wayfarers"- eight people who went on a vacation during the pandemic. We had planned to walk the Camino in June 2020, but when international travel was mostly suspended, we opted for Colorado instead.

I exited the truck and immediately felt emotion. A thickness in my throat, holding back tears for which I knew not the cause. Being in the company of friends and in this majestic place, Colorado National Monument, I was repeatedly overcome with emotion. My emotions—and tears—seeped out, not uncontrollably, but without my permission.

With each hike, each view, and each moment there was an emotional release. I didn't understand it at the time, I believe it was my soul releasing the grief of George's absence, who was already gone.

* * *

Journal Entry – January 2021 (Three years after his death)

I awoke calm, almost at peace. Stretching my ankles and wiggling my toes, I noticed I did not have the familiar sensation of tears beginning to well in my chest. I grinned almost imperceptibly.

My dream flooded back into my consciousness… it was George; he was talking to me. I saw his face, held it in my hands, and we were laughing together. It all came rushing back, and the emotion erupted from my throat and out through my eyes. It was so sweet, so tender. He closed his eyes as his "visit" was ending, and he let me know that he missed me.

The visit felt so real.

He had always been able to ground my spirit. The wonderful feeling of comfort grounded me.

* * *

The Rhythm of Peace

Finding the new rhythm for your life…that is the incredible challenge after experiencing the loss of a loved one. How a person finds peace within this challenge is as unique as their fingerprints–a personal rhythm of grief.

Remember: give yourself time to feel the grief; look for the bubbles that will lead you to the light; reach out for help as you need it; and keep counting to ten.

You can do anything for ten seconds.

* * *

It was Cindy, my courageous, trailblazing sister, who first gave me the ten-second mantra. I doubt she knew that those words would become my lifeline, guiding me and helping me rise again. I am and always will be profoundly and forever grateful.

* * *

Epilogue

I'm still counting to ten.

Grief no longer storms into my life as it once did. It no longer knocks me to my knees without warning or steals the breath from my lungs. Instead, it lives beside me—sometimes quiet, sometimes stirring, always present. It has become a companion of sorts, a reminder of the love that shaped me, broke me open, and taught me how to stand again.

The world I live in now is not the world I knew with George, nor is it the one I inhabited when loss gutted my soul. It is something new and woven together with memory, healing, forgiveness, humor, and the kind of courage you only discover when you have no choice but to move forward.

I still talk to George most days. Sometimes I tell him what the kids are doing. Sometimes I ask for patience. Sometimes I simply say, "I miss you." I no longer anticipate a reply, yet I somehow feel heard. His presence is stitched into the blueprint of my days—soft, steady, familiar. Love doesn't evaporate. It transforms.

I have learned that healing is not the closing of a chapter, it is the widening of a heart. It is learning to carry joy and sorrow together, to laugh without guilt, to cry without fear, and to trust that a life can be reshaped–even after it has been shattered.

There are moments when grief still surprises me: a song, a memory that rises uninvited. But instead of bracing myself, I now allow it. Tears come, and they go. Love comes, and it stays.

My life continues to grow in directions I never expected– new home, new experiences, new love, new peace. I honor George not by standing still in the shadow of loss, but by living fully in the light that remains. This, I believe, is what he would want.

To you, the reader who has walked beside me in these pages:

I hope you have discovered something of your own strength, your own rhythm, your own permission to grieve exactly as you need to. There is no timeline, no map, no correct way to mourn. There is only the next breath, the next step, the next ten seconds.

Grief will change you.

Let it.

And then let life change you again.

You can do anything for ten seconds.

And eventually–those ten seconds become a life worth living.

Acknowledgments

The list of people I want to thank for their love and support is tremendous, and it brings me to my knees with gratitude.

* * *

First and foremost, I want to thank my husband, George Fredrick Braun, for the incredible and indelible way he loved me. Without his love, this journey with grief would not exist as my inspiration.

* * *

Pre-readers: Lisa Bailey, Cindy Diven, Colleen Hart, Corinne Keller, Anne Morris, and Tracy Young.

The time you dedicated, and the delivery of your well-thought-out suggestions were invaluable to this project.

* * *

Editors: Corinne Keller, Anne Morris, and Tracy Young.

I will never forget the vulnerability I felt the first time I placed my manuscript in your hands… Thank you for your loving and brutal honesty.

* * *

Original artwork

- Special thanks to Lexi Braun. I met Lexi about a month before she turned nine years old, in 1993. Lexi created the original artwork for my memorial tattoo to honor her father; it has now been adapted for my book cover. Your creative talent and drive never cease to amaze me.

- Thank you, Myda Iamiceli, for adding your artistic eye and adapting Lexi's original artwork to create the beautiful cover of my first book.

* * *

A second note of acknowledgment to Anne Morris. Thank you for helping bring this story to life through the audiobook. From music years ago to this moment, your presence in my life has come full circle in the most meaningful way.

* * *

I cannot conclude without thanking my daughter, Emma Jean, and Dusty, our faithful companion. Emma Jean was still in high school when I began writing *The Rhythm of Grief.* She has lived through many hours of hearing my ideas, being asked for her opinion, and putting up with my voice interrupting the quiet of the house hour by hour, as I read aloud the new passages to make sure the flow of the book made sense. She's incredibly patient, and I rely on her opinion.

Dusty is my miniature schnauzer. He's a scruffy, salt-and-pepper, fourteen-pound cutie pie. He has patiently curled up next to me, waiting for me to take a break and go for walks. George picked him to be our companion, he chose well.

* * *

A Final Message to George

My Honey Bunny,

If there is a way for my words to reach beyond this world and into wherever your light now lives, let this reach you.

Thank you.

Thank you for loving me with the kind gentleness that softened every hard edge of my life. Thank you for the laughter that glued us together, the routines that became rituals, the quiet mornings, the coffee moments–even the one you just pretended to drink. Thank you for raising our children with me, for showing them what unconditional love looks and feels like, for teaching us all how to be better versions of ourselves.

I hope you know–truly know–that I did my best. Even when I stumbled, even when fear and exhaustion made me sharp, my heart was always trying to keep pace with the depth of my love for you. I carry both the beauty and ache of our life with me every day.

You asked not to be forgotten.

You aren't. You will never be.

You live in our stories, in our photographs on the wall, in the way the kids laugh, in the way I pause before every big decision and ask myself, What would George do? You live in the ashes held in glass, in the cranes I folded until my fingers ached, in the breath I take before I count to ten.

Your presence is in the simplest parts of my life—"blowing out" the lights at night, finding dryer sheets in the folded laundry, a rooster figurine, the quiet moments when I feel most like myself. I am who I am because you loved me, and because I loved you back with everything I had.

I want you to know this too:

I am living.

I am changing.

And I am okay.

I picture you in a classroom somewhere in heaven—learning about where you are and organizing everything so that it's better for everyone else. It's time you get out from behind the student desk and begin to teach. That's what you always did best.

I will love you the rest of my days, and more.

Rest easy, my Honey Bunny.

I've got us from here.

Your Honey Bunny, Betty Jean

Reader Reflections

These reflections were shared by early readers of this story.

"This book affected me in ways I hope will stay with me."
— Tabitha Benway

"I read the book in one day because once I started, I could not stop."
— Patsy Conlon

"You show how someone can persevere without saying, 'I can do it, so can you.'"
— Michael Gamble, Middle School Principal

"This really is a handbook, even though you say it is not."
— Betsy Berry

"Grief changes you in ways you don't fully understand until you've lived it."
— JoAnne Rice, Florida Division of State Fire Marshal

Elizabeth "Betty Jean" Braun is a retired firefighter / paramedic, former science teacher, and the author of *The Rhythm of Grief: A Memoir of Love, Loss, and Learning to Breathe Again.* Her life has been shaped by service, family, and a long habit of reflection through journaling that began in her teenage years.

For twenty-three years, she shared a marriage grounded in love, humor, and mutual respect with her husband, George. When George was diagnosed with cancer, Betty Jean became his caregiver while continuing to balance work, motherhood, and the emotional weight of impending loss. Throughout his illness—and after his death—she documented her experience in journal entries that captured grief as it unfolded in real time.

Her memoir weaves personal reflection with insight drawn from years in emergency services, exploring themes of grief, trauma, forgiveness, resilience, and the quiet beauty that can emerge from heartbreak. She writes honestly about the messiness of sorrow and the courage required to live again without leaving love behind.

Betty Jean believes grief has a rhythm unique to every person and that healing does not mean forgetting. Through storytelling, she hopes to offer companionship to those who are grieving—and permission to laugh, remember, and breathe again.

She lives in Florida, where she continues to honor George's memory, nurture her family, and count to ten when life feels overwhelming.

www.ingramcontent.com/pod-product-compliance
Lightning Source LLC
Chambersburg PA
CBHW031050160726
47991CB00005B/2098